IMPROBABLE MD:

FROM THE BAYOU TO THE BOARDROOM

Published by Hazel Eyes Press, LLC, Springfield, IL

Library of Congress Control Number: 2022914743

ISBNs
979-8-9861722-0-0 Hardcover
979-8-9861722-3-1 Paperback
979-8-9861722-1-7 Digital
979-8-9861722-2-4 Audio

Cover Design: Sergey Myshkovskiy
Interior Formatting: Olivier Darbonville
Editing and Proofreading: Erika's Editing

IMPROBABLE MD

FROM THE
BAYOU TO THE
BOARDROOM

BY DEREK J. ROBINSON, MD

To my patients, who have given me
the privilege of a lifetime to care
for them as their physician.

To my many mentees who, over the
years, have inspired me to strive toward
being a better example of God's grace.

To my readers, who I hope will find
encouragement in these pages.

was known for its academic excellence. Unfortunately, the school refused to take me: the administration at South Highlands didn't feel I was a good fit for their program since my father didn't live with us. Undoubtedly, my mother was devastated at this news. Her first real engagement with our city's school system had marked me as deficient and lacking potential for academic excellence. South Highlands didn't care that I was a smart, curious child who loved to ask questions, nor did they care that I saw my father almost once a week. They merely saw the circumstances of my birth and dismissed me.

To understand why my education was so important to my mother, it's necessary to know where she comes from. She's a child of sharecroppers, and both her parents were of African and Native American ancestry. Her father was born in 1888, and her paternal grandparents were both born into slavery. Her dad, who was over sixty years old when she was born, lived through the post-Reconstruction era, the terrorism of lynchings, the rise of Jim Crow, and the Civil Rights movement of the 1960s. My mother's mother, Big Momma, was my grandfather's third wife, and she was thirty-three years her husband's junior.

My grandparents didn't have wealth or many material possessions to offer their children, but they had their faith, their love, and each other to sustain them. They didn't have electricity in the home until my mother was seven years old, and indoor plumbing wasn't installed until several years after that. My mom and her siblings all shared beds, but they stayed warm and cozy under their quilts. Their two-room home was tight on space, yet there were always plenty of biscuits to go around. When she was in first grade, my mom went to school at our church, where the family worshipped. In their tattered clothes, she and her siblings would set off daily to school on the school bus that took the older kids into the city for high school. As one of the younger children in the family, my mother benefited from having older sisters and brothers to tutor her, and she thrived academically. Her educational path might have ended after twelfth grade, save for the advice of a few angels disguised as guidance counselors at her de facto segregated high school; they encouraged her to continue her studies, and she became the second in the family to go to college. Without their help, she probably wouldn't have overcome the extreme poverty of her childhood.

Because my mother was determined to find a good school for me, I landed at Judson Fundamental Magnet, a great elementary school where I forged what would become lifelong relationships—even today, I remain connected to friends from those early years. While I did fine academically, and even though I had a healthy self-confidence, elementary school was not a walk in the park. We used to receive these little slips of paper with a stamp showing our behavior—our "grade" for the day could be a star, a smiley face, or a frown. I got my fair share of frowns for talking too much in class, and according to my mom, during my first few years in school, she came to expect a call from my teacher on the first day of each school year. I think a good amount of my antics stemmed from my curiosity. For example, a replica of a human skeleton, with its many bones, was on display in the back of the school's science room; until my teacher admonished me for touching it, "Mr. Skeleton" and I often shook hands. I can now laugh at the notion, but I'm sure these incidents were frustrating for my mom, especially after working so hard to place me in a good school.

Science and math were my favorite subjects, but I also liked art. In science, I found our exploration of the solar system captivating. In fifth grade, I was excited when our homework was to create a model of the solar system, and I used spray-painted Styrofoam balls, cut in half and affixed to a poster board, to represent the sun and each of the planets. Unfortunately, just after I turned the model in, the nation faced the tragedy of the Space Shuttle Challenger explosion, and shock and dismay spread through my class. We knew that a teacher was one of seven people on board, and I worried that I could lose one of the teachers I admired in such an accident. Moreover, because my mother periodically traveled for work, the Challenger explosion made me worry that perhaps a plane she was traveling on could crash as well. Thankfully, time after time, she would arrive back home safely, which eventually soothed my fears.

Outside of academics, some of my fondest elementary memories include field day (dunking booths, sprints, bean bag races), singing in the school choir, taking turns raising the flag on the flagpole, serving as a safety patrolman (Safety patrolmen acted as crossing guards. We got to wear an orange belt with a triangular buckle, and we'd stop traffic so students could safely cross to the sidewalk.), and being in the Cub Scouts. Of all of these, I enjoyed Cub Scouts the most, as we would meet after school and do all kinds of fun activities.

My all-time favorite activity as a young boy was going to the local campgrounds for a camping trip. I would usually go with my friend Shaun and his family; his dad was active in our Cub Scout den, and he really enjoyed doing outside activities with us. When we weren't at the campground, from time to time, we would raise money for the local cystic fibrosis organization because Shaun's younger brother had the condition. As a kid, I don't recall observing symptoms of the disease in Shaun's brother, but I do remember hearing he might not live a long life. As a physician, I now have a better understanding of the challenges the family must have faced, especially in light of the limited technology in the 1980s, and as a father I understand why Shaun's dad took such joy in chaperoning our camping trips.

As much as my mother valued education, I was also raised in the church, as my family has long practiced the Christian faith. Deep faith carried our ancestors across chattel slavery, through emancipation, past segregation, and into contemporary times. For my family, our place of worship was the Starlight Baptist Church, which was founded in 1874. Starlight Baptist was a country church out in the sticks, and for many years, the building didn't have air conditioning. Fans would blow hot air from the outside into the hot church, which did little to cool us off. We didn't have a fancy choir, drums, or an organ to accompany our praises to God, but the choir always stayed in key and on beat, in synch with the stomping boots of my older cousin, who was the choir director for many years. With an understanding of God's grace and mercy, our elders bellowed out old hymns, which were reminiscent of the spirituals that nourished the souls of their ancestors as they toiled on plantations, during devotion time. Many weeks I watched in awe as Big Momma would catch the Spirit and dance and shout in church for as long as she was able. When I was very young, it bothered me when the ushers would come to walk her outside to cool off. I honestly didn't know what those men were doing to her, but my grandmother seemed upset when they came, and I didn't want anyone messing with her.

Of all my experiences in the church, I especially remember the baptisms. Water was in limited supply in our church because we relied on a well (which produced hard water that left the sinks and toilets with rust-colored stains), and we didn't have a baptismal pool, so baptisms took place in the woods instead. Candidates for baptism would get ready in the small church bathrooms and emerge draped in white robes and head wraps. The pastor and deacons would don their chest-level rubber waders and lead the congregation across the road, through a barbed-wire fence, and down a trail to a hidden pond. Parishioners would sing "Take Me to the Water" as we made our way through the woods. While some deacons were always in the water to assist with the baptisms, a few were stationed along the banks to watch for snakes, alligators, and other creatures that might be lurking in the water.

Every Sunday began with Sunday school class before the main service, and every Saturday evening my mother, who taught the adult class, would quiz me on the upcoming lesson to ensure that I was prepared for the next morning. My older cousin ran the kids' class and gave out candy-orange slices if we did a good job with our recitations. Sweets were always a strong incentive for us kids; it's amazing how much time I spent soliciting pieces of candy from every old lady with a purse. (I think we kids all figured out who had the good stuff and hit them up regularly.) I learned about Christ in Sunday school, but even beyond the religious principles, these classes were an educational training ground for me: reading comprehension, critical thinking, and public speaking were all an integral part of our lessons.

Like many churches, we often had programs that coincided with major holidays. This meant that young people would be given a poem or short speech to give during the program. Our youth director would assign a selection to each of us a few weeks beforehand, and we were expected to learn it by heart, or close to it. One of my mother's pet peeves was a cold reading of a poem from a child who had clearly made no effort to memorize the words, and so she made sure her son was ready to speak in front of the congregation; the night before any special program, I found myself standing in front of the faux fireplace in our living room, repeating my poem until it was perfect. As I got older, the poems got longer, but mom's standards and expectations did not change.

By the time I was a teenager, our church population had become smaller as some members, including a few of my own family, left Starlight Baptist for more modern churches. When I was sixteen, I became the permanent teacher for one of our youth classes; I had to learn how to conduct a thirty-minute class and keep my students well-behaved enough not to get us in trouble with the pastor for being too rowdy. It was during these years that our church was able to install air conditioning, which was a tremendous relief. It offered us respite from the heat and humidity, of course, but air conditioning came with another benefit: since the windows could now remain closed during the summer, we had fewer wasps flying into the church. Winter mornings were another story, though. As a youth teacher and one of the first people to arrive for Sunday school, I got plenty of practice lighting the church's propane space heaters. I would first check the external propane tank's level, then turn on the gas; by the time our seniors arrived, there were a few warm spots in the church waiting for them.

Our pastor chose every second Sunday as Youth Sunday, and I was afforded the chance to serve as superintendent of our entire Sunday school service. This was my first leadership position, and even though I was a teenager, the adults respected the role I was in; when I called on them in classes, they all started their responses with, "Brother Superintendent Robinson." The elders of the church encouraged me every step of the way, and they often reminded me that I didn't have to be a perfect leader as long as I put forth the effort and came prepared. "The elders will help you carry the tune, but they can't fix the wrong words," they would say. This taught me an important lesson in how I should govern myself in working with those who were more experienced than me, for I was humbled by the wisdom the elders shared.

The Starlight Baptist Church may not have been perfect, but its shortcomings were superficial, and year after year I was enriched with love from people who celebrated my faith, fostered my potential, and charged me with the responsibility of carrying forward the legacy of my ancestors—ancestors who never had the privilege of going to the many places that were destined for me. Here in my church home, I was encouraged to become my full and true self, protectively shaded by the elders and the congregation, in a world deeply rooted in love, faith, and hope.

CHAPTER 2

Swimming Across (Racial) Lanes

As far back as I can remember, I have always had a love for swimming and the water. Fear of the water was not uncommon in my community, but I delighted in my summertime swimming lessons at the George Washington Carver YMCA on Hearne Ave, as well as at other city pools. Each season, my mother signed me up for these classes through my day care. She wanted me to swim because she never had a chance to learn; growing up, her rural community didn't have a pool, and it's not likely that her parents could have financed lessons to begin with. My father, too, encouraged me to swim—he never took swimming lessons as a child, but he was adventurous enough to have learned with his friends and siblings on a local bayou. I looked forward to these classes each year, and seeing the water filled to the rim of the pool, with sunlight reflected in its stillness, excited me over and over.

I was twelve years old when I dove into the world of competitive swimming almost on a whim. One hot spring afternoon, I was in the car with my dad when I pleaded with him to stop at the Southside Swim Club, home of the City of Shreveport Swim Team (COSST). We'd passed the club many times—it was located across the road from our local mall—but I'd never been inside. I couldn't hide my excitement when my dad pulled the car into the parking lot. When we then entered the club's main grounds, I was in awe of the three sunlit pools, which I had been unable to see from the street.

The largest of the pools was fifty meters long, with eight lanes for swimmers, and it was much bigger than any pool I had ever seen. Swimmers stroked up and down the sun-kissed lanes as their coach Butch stood behind the blocks, sporting a straw hat. I quickly introduced myself to him and expressed my interest in trying out for the team. Of course, at twelve years old, I had absolutely no inkling of the commitment I was making in that moment, nor could I have been aware of the hard work, discipline, and dedication that would be required of me if I were to swim competitively.

That day, Butch invited me to take part in the team's upcoming practice, and soon I would learn just how far behind the other swimmers I truly was. When we returned, he instructed me to swim a lap. I dipped into the cold water and began to stroke and kick down my lane, but as I reached the other end of the pool, fatigue was already setting in; meanwhile, the other swimmers gracefully and effortlessly swam right around me. To his credit, rather than placing me with kids my age, Butch directed me to the group of younger swimmers practicing in the indoor, twenty-five-yard pool. There I was, a middle-school student in the lane with kids who were probably in second and third grades—including Butch's son, who despite being so young was a third-generation competitive swimmer. This was a challenging start for me because I couldn't blend in as I figured things out. I was older than the others, my swimming skills needed refinement, and I was the only Black swimmer in the pool. While I loved swimming and tried not to get discouraged, I initially wasn't sure that COSST was for me. I'm sure I made some basic improvement in my first few weeks, but change can be hard to see in the moment, and I wondered if I would ever catch up to the kids my age.

The Southside Swim Club was a special place. It was the preeminent training site for competitive swimming in the city, and kids from all over Shreveport were members. Its late founder Jack Jordan is credited with bringing competitive swimming to Louisiana in the 1950s, and Butch, his son, took over as head coach after finishing college. Although he wasn't actively coaching when I was on the team, Jack was always in his office taking care of club business and promoting competitive swimming across Louisiana. As if he were coaching us himself, he knew the stats of every team member—he was always on top of our best times, knew which of us had made the cut for various meets, and always had encouraging words to say. Whenever I stopped into his office, which was often, he was warm and welcoming, and we talked about the day's news or the latest technology. He had a passion for computers, was a huge fan of the National Rifle Association, loved his family dearly, and was proud that two of his grandkids were on the team. Over the years, I became so close to Jack that my mom, who had access to various tech products through work, would always offer him the latest cordless phones at a discount. It's impossible for me to gauge how many kids he fostered and encouraged over his decades at the club, but I'm sure the number must have been in the thousands. To this day, the club and team stand as part of Jack's enduring legacy in Shreveport.

After I joined COSST, it wasn't long before I began to notice the swim team's logo on some of the apparel of my classmates, yet our paths didn't cross at the club because I had so much catching up to do. I was starting at the bottom, and it seemed like it would take a miracle for me to rise to the top. Over the next two years, I practiced five times a week as I developed my skills, built my endurance, and worked my way onto the team with kids my age. I had an innate drive to compete but, along the way, the journey was a struggle. Progress would not come easily or as the result of growth spurts. I adjusted my diet so that I'd have energy enough to endure the rigorous training. I prepared myself mentally, grounded in my faith, with the principles of sports psychology. I learned how to push myself beyond my physical and mental limits, and in time, I came to genuinely appreciate the importance of good swim technique.

While I always had a relationship with my dad, we became much closer when I started swimming. As the owner of a small bail bond business, my father had the flexibility to make his own hours, and surprisingly, he stepped in and took me to my practices and meets. This fortified our relationship in ways that I never imagined, although we did have some bumps and bruises along the way. His words of love and encouragement often didn't feel that way; I couldn't always use them to uplift my spirits on a bad day or validate the progress of my efforts. Instead, they were blunt and heavy, loaded with the best he had to offer. He was from an older school of thought and believed that direct acknowledgment of progress would weaken performance. He also didn't have the swimming jargon quite right, which confused me even more. When my dad said, "Your hands have to slice through the water and raise your body up," what he really meant was, "You need to keep your elbows high, extend the reach of your stroke, and have a powerful catch on the water as you pull back towards your waist." When I talked about this with my mom, she always tried to translate his words for me, but I'm not sure that it made me feel any better. Even still, my dad would often sit on the deck during my practices, and, as he was also one of our parish's elected commissioners, time at the club gave him the chance to interact with parents from the business and criminal justice communities. On the one hand, I think my dad was proud I was swimming with the kids of respected members of the community; on the other, watching me struggle was probably frustrating.

Apart from swimming at the club, in my pre-varsity years, I competed in our city's summer league meets, which were held at swim clubs in different parts of the city each week. These were small adventures for me during my first summers on the team; growing up I thought I had seen all of the city's pools, but that was just my narrow perspective. Clearly there were more pools out there, and I approached each with the same excitement. These meets were important confidence boosters for me, as I was able to compete with other swimmers my age and often win races. Winning showed that I was making progress, and as an added benefit, my dad could stick his chest out a bit as well. Although I knew that the real competition was back at my home swim club, I celebrated those small wins because they encouraged me to continue working hard.

Starting at the bottom wasn't the only challenge I faced on the team: I also had to navigate the murky waters of race relations in my hometown, which is a former capital of the Confederacy. While the "Whites Only" signs of our cast-iron, Jim-Crow past were no more, the legacy of segregation seemed to be ever-present in my experience—if I'd tried to join the team even twenty-five years earlier, I would've been prohibited from the pool by law. For about three years, I was the only Black swimmer on a team of more than one hundred strong, and at times this felt like an alternate reality. I couldn't simply blend in with others when I fell short of my personal goals, and I was constantly under a spotlight. Even in my dad's eyes, there was nowhere I could hide, and during my early days, I know it pained him when I fell behind in practice or finished last in a race. When I looked at the photos of past teams that lined the wall of Butch's office, I couldn't find a face that looked like mine, and I may have been the first African American swimmer on our team. When attending meets across the state, I stood out even more, as we would only occasionally see one other Black family. Culturally, I also felt like an outsider, both in the pool and around the club. It was the 1990s, and in my neighborhood, we were jamming to Tupac Shakur, A Tribe Called Quest, Outkast, and Biggie Smalls; yet I remember going to a party at a team member's home where everyone was country line-dancing to the Boot Scootin' Boogie. I eventually caught onto the steps, but I certainly hadn't come prepared with cowboy hats and boots like a few of my teammates. I often felt divides like this keenly; many of my teammates and I attended the same school, but otherwise our lives were separate. We lived on different sides of town, went to different places of worship, practiced different customs, and had different cultural perceptions.

On several occasions, I heard racial slurs at the pool. I vividly recall an instance where I confronted the younger brother of two of my varsity teammates when he referred to African Americans as niggers. He "defended" himself, explaining, "I'm not talking about you, you're not like the rest of them." Episodes like this really stung, and if I hadn't had such a strong sense of purpose imparted to me by my mother and our church, they could've done real damage. Instead of internalizing the hurt, I tried to find the lesson buried beneath such ignorance. After all, there was no committee on diversity and inclusion to receive my complaint, and I was confident that if I quit, the team would be just fine without me. Ultimately, each of these injuries reminded me not to confuse kindness with acceptance. I had to understand that while some swimmers and parents were bold enough to overtly push their rudeness and ignorance onto me, there was a critical mass of silent others who felt the same.

I wanted to compete, and racism wouldn't stop me. I was especially mindful of my friendships with white girls on the team and how those friendships might be perceived at the pool—any hint of interracial dating could rankle my teammates or their parents—and a few times some of these girls quietly conveyed to me that they were wary of the same. And the reality for some swimmers was that their mandate from their parents was not to finish behind the Black boy in any race. I was swimming across racial lanes, and there was no one to mentor me on this journey; my dad and many of the other parents grew up during a time in Louisiana where facilities were racially segregated, especially swimming pools. However, this was not the 1950s or 1960s, but rather the late 1980s and into the 1990s. Perhaps the benefit of youth is the optimistic belief that you can overcome adversity and discrimination. This empowered me to not be discouraged by the past. Little did I know that building my self-confidence and cross-cultural competency through navigating race relations at the club would prepare me for many similar experiences as an adult.

Today, as I reflect on more recent experiences, despite some progress, I must say too many attitudes in our society have not changed. In the summer of 2020, I read articles in *Big Easy Magazine*[1] and on *Refinery29*[2] about a members-only swim club in Vacherie, Louisiana that ran a whites-only swimming pool; the club effectively denied Black people membership by placing them on a never-ending waiting list. Individuals quoted in the articles alleged that La Vacherie Swimming Club never had a Black member. In fact, one of the articles described how, in 2014, La Vacherie Swimming Club, part of River Parish Swim League, voted along with three other league-member clubs to expel the league's only racially diverse team, the Piranhas. It was sobering to read a more detailed article in the *L'Observateur*[3] about the expulsion of the Piranhas and how the vestiges of legal segregation are still alive and well, even as we approached the middle of the twenty-first century.

Despite my negative experiences at COSST, a small but memorable group of my teammates was very inclusive; I became friends with them outside of the club, and I felt welcome in their homes. I discovered that two of my teammates' fathers were physicians, one an oncologist and the other an endocrinologist. They were often on the pool deck serving as officials at our meets, and they were the first physicians I was able to spend time with outside of a clinical setting; they would talk to me about my growing interest in medicine. I learned that they treated patients *and* were engaged in medical research for various conditions, which initially surprised me because I didn't understand that practicing physicians could also be scientists. Both these doctors worked at LSU Health Shreveport, our local safety-net hospital where patients without

---

1 Big Easy Magazine: <https://bit.ly/3s5qXpY>
2 Refinery29: <https://r29.co/3KAKghk>
3 L'Observateur: <https://bit.ly/3vTy7yM>

private health insurance—including many of my family members—received care, and they helped me broaden my understanding of public/private medicine. Their influence on me was significant; later, during my first year of college, they both aided me in obtaining a summer research internship. That internship strengthened my basic scientific knowledge and gave me my first understanding of the importance of laboratory research in improving medical care. That same summer, another former teammate's father (who worked at the hospital adjacent to the research center as a certified registered nurse anesthetist) allowed me to shadow him in the operating room caring for pediatric burn patients undergoing skin grafting. These were important motivators; they helped push me toward medical school.

While my years at the club began with a simple interest in swimming, the experience taught me lessons about race and racism, class, religion, and the difference between being tolerated and being truly included. My time there also etched into my brain the values of discipline, teamwork, and perseverance. These lessons have served me well in all aspects of my life. I appreciate those who welcomed and supported me on the team during a time when diversity and inclusion were not mainstream; surely, we are all better adults today because of the journey we took together. When we embraced our differences—both in and out of the pool—with authenticity and understanding, we helped create the foundation for the type of societal change that we see this generation of young people fostering today.

CHAPTER 3

One Son, Two Families

"Anything worth having is worth working hard for," my mother often said. Like any child, I had dreams about what I would be when I grew up, yet I also understood at an early age that whatever I pursued, I would have to work hard to earn the opportunity. Nothing but my family's love and God's grace would ever be handed to me.

My aunt Peggy, the first of my mother's family to go to college, reinforced this idea with a story she shared with me many times over the years. When she was a student at Grambling State University, which is about two hours east of Shreveport by Greyhound bus, her parents didn't have much money to give her, but they supported her in their own way. This came in the form of care packages in the mail; more specifically, Big Momma would send her egg sandwiches. Whenever a package arrived, my aunt would privately open the pungent box, the inside of which was not a pretty sight after transit. Yet those mangled sandwiches represented the love the family had to offer. While I grew up hearing this story told now and again, I didn't truly appreciate its depth until years later when I was in medical school. One year, when I was too overwhelmed with my studies to travel home for Thanksgiving, I found myself the recipient of a medium-sized and well-taped-up package marked "Urgent." I lost no time in opening it, and inside I found a dry-ice-packed Styrofoam chest containing a stuffed, beautifully browned turkey. This taste of home was my godfather Martell's love in action, a twenty-first-century version of Big Mama's egg sandwiches.

My mother's love came largely in the form of strong morals and ethics, as she took every chance to ingrain in me the importance of hard work and education. One incident that stands out happened when I was about twelve years old. My mother needed to place some items in her safety deposit box at the bank, and she took me along with her. While we were in the vault, she handed me an envelope to open. Dated in the 1960s, the letter was from Southern University and A&M College in Baton Rouge, and it informed her that she'd been awarded a full, four-year scholarship; I believe the amount was eight-hundred dollars. She told me that she was the valedictorian of her high school class and had originally planned to attend a community college for an associate's degree. A guidance counselor pushed her sights higher, and the result was now having a multigenerational impact. As I read the letter, I understood the lesson my mother was teaching me: I needed to stay focused on performing well in school so I could open the door to opportunity by going to college. The responsibility to achieve was mine, but my mom paved the way and was willing to walk the journey with me.

Other family members showed me the way to education through their actions. When I was about ten years old, my uncle Robert began attending night school, between his day job and his night job, at a local Bible college; he eventually earned an associate's degree in theology.

Later, my aunt Ruth, who was the youngest of the twenty-one siblings, also achieved her bachelor's degree. While neither my mom nor her siblings who attended college became wealthy, education greatly enhanced their lives, which, in turn, allowed them to become anchors for the family.

As I look back over the years, there were places I visited where my potential was fostered, even when I was too young to see it in myself. For example, my childhood barber, the late Jerry Bowman of Jerry's #1 Barbershop, always encouraged me. Like so many of his customers, I can still hear his welcoming voice in my head: "Hold up everybody, now we've just had a future president of the United States walk in the door," he often shouted when I arrived. Whenever I would visit the shop for a haircut, Jerry would call me by one of my affirming nicknames—Doctor, Mr. President—and if my uncle Robert were in the shop (as he often was,) he'd chime in with supporting words. I would often spend many hours in the clamorous shop waiting on my cut, but the cumulative experience taught me that there was a higher expectation for kids of my generation, born in the post-Civil-Rights era, to pursue excellence.

On the maternal side of my family, my uncle Robert provided the strongest male influence in my life, and I don't really recall a part of my childhood without him. His oldest daughter and I were the same age and often played together. He was one of my mom's younger brothers, and they jogged together and ran five-kilometer races. Like many in my family, uncle Robert was a man of faith and served as a minister at his church. During vacation Bible school, which was held in the summer, he would drive his church's van through the city while blasting gospel songs over the loudspeakers. My cousin and I would sometimes ride in the back and sing along to, "We Are the World" and other songs. We didn't have enough self-awareness to be embarrassed by our lack of musical talent, and undoubtedly, we were enjoying a snack from the church as we sang.

A former marine, uncle Robert read meters for the city's water department. He got plenty of exercise going from property to property, and he knew the city very well. However, although he worked hard, his job didn't pay him enough to raise a family on, so he would often moonlight as a janitor at a local motel. Despite his long hours, I don't recall him ever turning down a request for us to go fishing together. He had an old car with a perpetually broken air conditioner, and I could always find fishing poles in the trunk. Fishing was our favorite pastime together, and when we were out, he would always find a moment to encourage me to further my education. "Be sure you stay in school so you can get a good job. You don't want to have to work as hard as I do to make ends meet," he often advised me.

During the summers of my middle school years, I particularly remember uncle Robert stopping by my home on his lunch break so we could eat together. Back then, I loved to fry my bologna in the skillet for a tasty sandwich, but he would always boil his. As a kid this puzzled me because the boiled bologna didn't have that nice crispy taste, but as I grew older, I learned my uncle frequently had an upset stomach and needed to tenderize his meats for easy digestion. Back then, neither of us could have known just how serious his upset stomachs were.

Unlike many of his brothers, uncle Robert wasn't averse to seeking medical care, and in subsequent years, he began going to doctors for evaluations. As a veteran, he primarily went to the VA medical center. At that time, the VA in our town didn't have a reputation for high-quality care, but treatment there was affordable and accessible as a benefit of his service to the nation. He also had private health insurance through the city, and when the VA couldn't help him, he began seeing in-network doctors at a local hospital. Despite all these visits, he could never get the issue with his stomach resolved—it seemed as though his complaints weren't taken seriously, and tests were rarely performed. My family and I wondered if my uncle was getting the care that he needed; his insurance wasn't accepted at one of the better local hospital systems (where my mother and I went for care), and this severely curtailed his options for treatment. Even as a child, I understood there were vast disparities in our healthcare system, and I suspected more could've been done for him.

It wasn't too long before uncle Robert began losing weight and having difficulty swallowing. At that point, he was diagnosed with stomach cancer, which had already spread to various organs and had begun to narrow his esophagus. This was devastating news for our family, but he was such a man of faith. Frequently sharing the wisdom of scripture, uncle Robert sought to encourage us in the Lord, even as he lost his taste for his favorite foods, started losing his hair from chemotherapy, and began withering away. Yet his faith was answered when, while still in treatment, his second daughter was born. He called her his miracle child, and she brought new love and joy into his life when he needed it most.

Eventually, uncle Robert could hardly swallow, and he began taking many nutritional supplements. I tried some of the homeopathic drinks for myself; they didn't taste good, but I understood he was doing all he could to boost his energy. When he was in treatment, we spent a lot of time talking together, and he certainly wasn't bitter. A humble man, he was thankful for his many blessings, and all he wanted for his remaining days was quality time with his family.

I remember clearly the evening when I learned of my uncle's passing. My mom picked me up after swim practice, as she often did. At the time, I was learning to drive and had my learner's permit. I walked around to the driver's side of the car thinking I would get to drive home that day, but my mother told me no. A sense of dread hit me. I climbed into the passenger seat, and my mom told me that uncle Robert had passed away. I was heartbroken and speechless. On the one hand, I knew he was suffering tremendously, but on the other I'd been hoping for a miracle and praying that he would turn a corner. But now I had to face the reality and finality of the death of a man who was not only my uncle but my friend. At age forty-one, this husband, father of two daughters, brother to twenty siblings, and beloved member of the community had gone home too soon. He'd been a constant source of inspiration for me, it seemed like he had so much more life left for him to live, and those who were closest to him needed him so much. At the time, I believed good health was strongly correlated with access to high-quality healthcare, which I knew in my heart my uncle hadn't received. My interest in medicine was solidified by the time my uncle passed, but now my interest broadened: when I became a doctor, I would develop more and better access to quality care for my family and community.

Losing my uncle was the second death of a close family member to touch my young life. Big Momma, who had problems with her heart and lived with diabetes, passed when I was twelve. In the years before her death, I recall many trips to LSU Medical Center Shreveport, the old Confederate Memorial Medical Center, to visit her. Back then, children were rarely allowed to go up to the wards to visit patients, and I spent a lot of time in the waiting room. It seemed like the same receptionist was always on duty, and she only relented occasionally when I asked to go upstairs with my mom for the visit. When I was allowed upstairs, on the way to the elevators, we always passed a double-door with signs in red lettering that said, "Restricted Access" and "Emergency Room." I was too young then to fully understand the health challenges Big Momma was facing, but I could read those signs clear as day, and I was transfixed; I thought to myself, "One day I'll get to go back there." My curiosity about the ER stayed with me throughout my childhood years, and even now it's amazing to me that these two great losses, years apart and under very different circumstances, each propelled me toward medicine.

IT'S EASY TO LOOK AT THE LIVES OF OTHERS AND CONTEMPLATE HOW much better your life's journey might have been if you were born into different circumstances. Probably like you, I've had so many of these "the grass is always greener" episodes along the way, but perhaps the primary and most significant area where I experienced these feelings was my immediate family's structure. My parents both loved me, but as a child born out of wedlock, I was aware that my birth carried some sort of stigma. My father was fairly well known in our city and never "hid" me in any way—in fact, I bore such a resemblance to him that people in public would often point it out—but at the same time, I carried with me a sense of not having the wholeness that others enjoyed. As an adult, I now understand that being born to a single mother isn't at all unique, but when I was growing up, I felt it was my Achilles' heel.

My father was the oldest of five siblings from his mom and dad, and he also had a stepbrother who was much older. Like my mom, my father came from very humble beginnings. He was raised in The Bottoms, one of the poorest areas of Shreveport; his father was a US Navy veteran who'd served during World War II, and his mother was a housekeeper who, for many years, worked in the home of a prominent wealthy family. Given their meek beginnings, a college education was not in the cards for my father or his siblings, but as an adult my dad appreciated that more opportunities were open to those with a post-secondary education. As one of our parish's commissioners, he often encouraged young people to go to college, and as a father, he worked to ensure that all his children had access to a college education.

My dad was an ambitious bootstrapper who found his own success through hard work. He had a wife and four children of his own, and I was aware of this for most of my life. He spoke about them at times, and I wondered what it would be like to have relationships with them. Most of my friends in the neighborhood had siblings at home, and some had older, adult siblings, yet there was a void in my life. I didn't have an older sister or brother who could take me to the fair or the skating rink, and on those occasions when I got into a neighborhood scuffle, I didn't have anyone who unequivocally had my back. I had an interest in knowing my siblings, but outside of a few interactions with my brother, I never did meet them as a child. I don't recall pressing my dad much on this issue, and I sort of accepted things as they were. Looking back, I don't fault my dad; life is complicated sometimes, and we do our best to move forward.

I longed to spend more time with my dad, but even as a young child I knew this wasn't possible. When we were together, I was his son and I never felt any different, but even with some of my closest friends, I felt like I was regarded differently for not having my father at home. Most of the other kids in my middle- and working-class neighborhood had two parents at home, and whether it was true or not, I felt like I stuck out. As an adult, I see how easy it is to default to holding children accountable for the decisions or circumstances of their parents, but I was much too young, of course, to understand this growing up. Too many kids carry burdens like these as heavy weights, weights that impair their growth and ability to live up to their full promise.

When I was in middle school, my father became more involved in my daily life. This was partly due to my joining the swim team, but also because he began taking me on more fishing trips with my paternal grandfather, who I affectionately called Granddad. We'd haul our green, aluminum boat into the back of my father's truck and head out to various fishing holes in northwest Louisiana and east Texas. When we approached Texas, I would close my eyes and try to pinpoint the moment we crossed into the state—the roads were much smoother on this side of the border. Because we headed out so early in the morning, it wasn't uncommon for me to take a nap on the ride to our fishing hole, and Granddad would always manage to slip a few dollars into my pocket.

For shorter trips, one of our favorite Shreveport fishing and squirrel-hunting spots was 12 Mile Bayou, a tributary of the Red River. Fueled by the warm apple fritters we often bought on our drive, I was tasked with carrying the boat's motor down the bank to the river. From there, we would head out onto the water, and fishing with Granddad was always great fun because he knew just where I should drop my hook and stopper for a good haul. He preferred an old-school cane pole over a modern rod and reel, but his fishing instincts were as accurate as any modern sonar system. One time, Granddad had us set up by a tree that had fallen into the water, in a spot covered with leaves and other natural debris. I didn't think we could catch anything worthwhile there in the shallows, yet fish after fish bit my line. Catch after catch, we filled up our ice chest with white perch larger than a man's hand. On those kinds of trips, we brought home more fish than we could ever eat, but whatever Granddad had, his neighbors had too; he would simply make a call, and someone would drop by. Sometimes, as we unloaded the boat in his yard, those in the know would come up to his fence and check to see if we'd any luck.

I'd known Granddad all of my life, but it was our time together when I was a teenager that transformed him into my favorite fishing buddy. Other than our fishing trips, I remember him sitting on his front porch or tending to the fruit trees in his front yard. Like most men of his generation in the neighborhood, he was usually packing on any given day. In the pocket of his overalls (his daily "uniform"), he kept a gray, .38 caliber pistol wrapped up in a plastic Wonder Bread bag. Although his neighborhood was pretty rough, I don't recall Granddad having any major issues with crime, and I never saw him pull his gun on anyone or otherwise discharge it. I loved spending time with Granddad; during my teen years especially, I truly did value watching my father and Granddad together: there was nothing son wouldn't do for dad. My father would even drive to the watermelon patch and load one-hundred red- and yellow-meat watermelons onto his truck for Granddad to sell outside his home. To this day, any time I'm checking a watermelon's ripeness by thumping on its rind, I think about the trips and the time the three of us had together.

In spending more time with my dad, my relationship with him changed. Before I became a teenager, our relationship was mostly free of conflict, but now we butted heads sometimes—his way versus my way, impassioned (and loud) discussions, his disappointment in my early swimming performances—and while this could at times be difficult, our relationship developed a new layer of authenticity. I came to know my dad in a different, but still-loving, way, and I realized that our living situation was probably ideal for us—God's perfect wisdom. Swimming especially provided moments of conflict, and I'm not sure I would have continued striving to improve in the sport I loved so much if my dad and I had been together every day.

My unique family structure has taught me many important life lessons about the complexities of relationships and love, accountability for personal decisions made in private, planning for the long term, and the grace of God. I wasn't born into a traditional or perfect family, but I was born into a family that was perfect for my growth and development. Perceived disadvantages formed the basis of many core lessons. I learned through the examples of others, enabling me to make better decisions than I would've made otherwise. In the coming years, as I left home for college and medical school, I would come to rely on the life lessons imparted to me by those I loved.

CHAPTER 4:

Claiming My Shot

My high school years were memorable and filled with pride. I met some really bright people, and we shared some truly unique times together. Our school had the nation's largest Junior ROTC Program, and our resource officer, who was from the local sheriff's department, was the tallest law-enforcement officer in the country. During my senior year, our girls' basketball team ranked first in the nation, our boys' basketball team won the state championships, our football team went undefeated in the district, and our baseball team won the district championship.

C.E. Byrd High School, a Blue-Ribbon school, was one of the best in Shreveport, and oddly enough my journey to placement there began in sixth grade at Caddo Middle Magnet school. At the end of elementary school, all students were evaluated and then funneled into various junior high schools based on achievement. I was placed in the city's most competitive junior high school, which was well-resourced academically, especially in the arts and sciences. Theater, concert-band, jazz-band, and judo all helped me become a well-rounded and competitive student, but at the same time, junior high was the first time I became consciously aware of the disparities within our public school system. In the eighth grade, during a conversation with a younger neighborhood friend, I realized that his junior high was being given my school's old textbooks when we received new ones. (Back then, when you were assigned a textbook, you wrote your name on a list on the inside cover; my sixth-grade friend wound up with the same textbook I'd used two grades earlier.) This crystallized in my mind that the competitive landscape for entrance to the most selective public high schools was uneven. Even if a student in an under-resourced school excelled academically, their opportunities were more limited than those of peers in better-performing schools. I realized the long-term consequences of this were significant, and it made me appreciate my placement at Byrd.

Early in high school, I had some excellent teachers who encouraged their students while insisting on a high level of achievement. It was almost as if my mother was sitting behind the desk when I was in Mrs. Smith's Algebra I class. She was a smaller-statured Black woman with silver hair who was always clear about her expectations. Her smile conveyed love, but no one dared to misbehave during her lessons or show up to her classroom tardy. Just as importantly, she ensured that we had a solid understanding of algebra's basics. Because she set her standards high, I was compelled to develop good study habits from day one. She expected all students to take careful notes and work through the practice equations in the back of our textbook. (These equations would regularly show up on her tests, so we needed to know our stuff.) These habits prepared me for future courses in high school and beyond.

When it was time for Algebra II, I was ready to roll. Mrs. Grimm was a high-energy teacher who was fond of pop quizzes, and she made math really fun. She was a short-haired, blonde woman who chewed gum, kept her collar popped, always wore high heels, and played in a rock band during the weekends. With her dry-erase markers in hand, she would stand at the overhead projector marking up the transparencies as she taught. Every student in her class knew we each had a solid chance of getting called on to work a line of the equation and move the algebraic variables along a step further toward the answer. Like Ms. Smith, Mrs. Grimm cared about student success and went the extra mile to ensure that we were intellectually challenged and continually motivated. In fact, when we were in the final stages of preparing for our standardized ACT exams, she held weekend test-prep sessions, which I took advantage of with gratitude.

Throughout my K–12 years, there were precious few times when a Black man headed one of my classrooms. I remember them all well. In elementary school, it was Mr. Lamar who stimulated my interest in science. In middle school, it was Mr. Wayne in social studies and Mr. Keels, a genius musician, in band. During high school, there were two such men—Mr. Graham and Coach Crosby—who nurtured me not just as a student, but as a young Black man.

When I started my civics and free enterprise class with Mr. Graham, I wasn't entirely clear on what the content of the course would be, but it soon became one of the most consequential classes of my high school years. Mr. Graham looked like he could've been my older brother, but he taught with the maturity and wisdom of a seasoned educator. Byrd High School served students from affluent neighborhoods and economically challenged areas alike, and despite his having diverse students with varying perspectives, Mr. Graham challenged our thinking on topics of policy, civic responsibility, and equity. Fresh on the minds of my friends and me at the time was the infamous beating of Rodney

King by the Los Angeles Police Department. I'd read much about the police brutality of the Civil Rights era, but watching such a tragedy on TV cut deep into me, and my friends and I often felt dehumanized by the insensitive and intolerant, yet painfully casual, comments of some of our classmates. The King beating (March 1991) sparked conversations in class for the rest of my freshman year and well into the next academic year. Our emotions were raw, and during that time, we needed Mr. Graham. When the LA riots (spring, 1992) erupted after all LAPD members were acquitted of criminal charges in the King beating, Mr. Graham again shepherded us and guided us as we worked through our complex thoughts and feelings. In his own way, he ensured that young men like me were better prepared to navigate the challenges we would face in the future. Most notably, he encouraged us to pursue constructive solutions through careers that would improve the lives of others.

My relationship with Coach Crosby had a deep and lasting impact on my development as well. For one of my elective classes, I signed up for his computer programming class. Since my mother was a computer programmer and I had been around computers since elementary school, my expectations were set on an easy course. Instead, I discovered a new relationship with Coach Crosby. He made sure that I learned the basics of DOS programming, but what I didn't know was that he would later become my boss at my summer job.

When I started lifeguarding during the summer, I was initially assigned to one of the busiest and largest pools in the city, but I was later posted to a pool in an underserved, high-crime area. At that point, Coach Crosby asked that I be assigned to his staff at Cross Lake beach; once I was working in a safer location, he pulled me under his wing, and he even ensured that I had scheduling-flexibility enough to accommodate my swim practices and Sunday-morning church responsibilities. On days when business was slow at the beach, he imparted measured doses of wisdom about the adulthood I would soon face as we slapped down dominoes or played games of backgammon, always with classic rock playing in the background.

Through lifeguarding, I got my first taste of responsibility for the safety and well-being of others. I knew the water well and was a strong swimmer, but even still I was keenly aware that any pool can be a very dangerous place. I took my charge as a lifeguard very seriously: when parents dropped off their children, they expected them to return home safely. I was trained in CPR and knew what to do if called into action, and my skill in preventing injury in and out of the water became my greatest asset. While I never had any dramatic life-saving rescues, I did occasionally pull in a swimmer before they got into real trouble, and I often dressed the scraped elbows and knees of those who sustained minor injuries while at the beach. This was my job, and I found a deep satisfaction in helping those who were in immediate distress and keeping others safe. Looking back, although I couldn't have known it at the time, in some ways lifeguarding was preparing me for my future as an ER doctor—in both roles, I needed to keep a cool head, fall back on my training, and address any crisis situation with focus and urgency.

During my later high school years, as my interest in medicine solidified, I signed up for multiple advanced-placement classes in biology, chemistry, and history. I also enrolled in advanced math classes and took physics. During my senior year, I took both AP Chemistry and AP Biology II. My classes with Dr. Bazer and Ms. Williamson were extraordinarily fun, filled with adventure and high expectations. In particular, during my AP Biology II class, I was tasked with researching a medical condition for a project. Somehow, I made my way over to the medical library of our local university hospital and, being a generally curious student, I randomly picked up a medical journal from a shelf. As I flipped through the pages, an article about nuclear medicine caught my attention. This sounded very interesting to me—nuclear bombs and medicine—and I immediately needed to know more. While I quickly figured out that the word *nuclear* did not, in this context, refer to weapons, the article included references to cardiac perfusion, ejection fraction, and other terms with which I was unfamiliar.

When I got home that night and told my mother about the article, she directed me to a family friend named Wayne, who worked in cardiology, for help. I remembered Wayne from my childhood, back when he lived across the street from my elementary school. He'd been a part of my mom's jogging group, and our families had stayed connected over the years through special events at our respective churches. When I reached out to him to see if he could help me better understand the article's terms and clinical perspective, he was more than happy to share his knowledge. As a cardiovascular technician in a local heart catheterization lab, Wayne stood right next to the cardiologists during cath procedures, anticipating the needs of physician and patient alike when the seconds counted. He ensured that the right instruments were ready and available at a moment's notice, and he kept a close eye on patient monitors, watching for even the smallest change. As a result of his work, he had expertise in understanding diseases of the heart, the diagnostic tests commonly used in cardiology, and the treatments used for heart conditions.

Wayne took my lesson further by inviting me to observe a few procedures. I remember sitting in the monitor-filled control room of the cath lab, positioned behind the protective lead glass that filtered out radiation. (During heart-cath procedures, X-rays are used to monitor patient blood flow through the cardiovascular system.) Chill music from Pat Metheny filled the air as the doctors, nurses, technicians, and technologists each played their role in caring for the patient. This seemed like a cool place to work; it was fascinating to watch each procedure. After one of the catheterizations, Wayne told me that he once had dreams of becoming a physician and that he was the only Black male working on his team. Moreover, none of the cardiologists in the hospital were Black or African American, although many of the patients were. While he'd made his peace with not achieving his full dream, Wayne *had* carved out his own unique contributions to his field. Before we left the lab that day, he showed me several devices he had designed that were currently in use by the cardiology team. During a later visit to his home, he showed me several patent certificates for existing and future devices.

Wayne's example demonstrated to me a different way of achieving expertise in your field. History would later reveal to me that many bright individuals in medicine, individuals who looked like Wayne and supported leading physicians, were under-appreciated or un-recognized for their work or invention, including a true innovator from my home state. Vivien Thomas was a Black man who became a pioneer in cardiac surgery. He worked as an assistant in the animal-testing lab of Alfred Blalock, a Nobel-Prize-nominated physician. Through years of work in the lab, Thomas developed a surgical technique to treat the tetralogy of Fallot, a congenital heart defect in animals. When the procedure was deemed safe for humans, Thomas was instrumental in many surgeries; in the operating room, he would stand behind Blalock, answering the doctor's questions and coaching him throughout the procedure. Despite his talent and hard work, Thomas's name was intentionally left out of the May 1945 article in the *Journal of the American Medical Association* that described the successful surgical breakthrough. It wasn't until 1976 that Thomas was properly recognized for his decades-long contribution to cardiac surgical care.[4] [5]

IN MY SENIOR YEAR OF HIGH SCHOOL, AS GRANDDAD'S HEALTH BEGAN to fail, I often went to his home to help care for him. I felt in my heart that I was destined to become a physician, but as I fed him his meals, distributed his medicines, and repositioned him to guard against pressure sores, I found myself facing an internal conflict. I had a true desire to improve the health of the vulnerable and underserved, but I feared publicly claiming a dream I was unsure I could attain—in my mind, there was no clear road map to physicianship. No one in my family had ever gone to medical school, and I'd seen precious few doctors who looked like me in my lifetime. I'd been blessed to have a large, if somewhat nontraditional, support system around me, but for those family, friends, coaches, and mentors who believed in my potential, how could I let them down if I failed? I wasn't a quitter and didn't shy away from challenges, but even if I assumed that I had all the traits necessary for success, I wasn't sure I wanted to spend the next eleven-plus years of my life in school and training; after all, as a senior I was just finishing

---

4   The Washingtonian: <https://bit.ly/3OREoU4>
5   The Washingtonian: <https://bit.ly/3F3rXQI>

thirteen years of school, and if I went down this path, I would be nearly thirty years old before I could practice medicine independently. This was daunting to contemplate.

As my last year of high school entered its final months, I had to make a decision about my future and where I would go to college. I'd applied widely to four-year programs across the nation, and by the time spring came that year, I'd been accepted to more than forty schools, some with full or partial academic scholarships. Yet there was one university that stood out for its reputation of preparing Black and African American students for medical school, and it was right here in my home state: Xavier University of Louisiana. I had driven through its modest campus earlier in the year while in New Orleans for a swim meet; it hadn't knocked me off my feet. I had doubts about this small, Catholic, HBCU[6] being the school for me, especially as I'd applied to some of the most-recognized colleges in the nation. Fortunately, my mother remembered that one of her coworkers had a daughter who was a Xavier alum and was currently a practicing physician. At my mom's urging, I connected with this alum by phone, and our conversation stands out as a pivotal moment in my decision-making process. She told me, "Attending Xavier will better prepare you to get into medical school than any other university in the country. If you go to Xavier now, you'll have the option to attend any of those other universities for medical school." Leaning on the wisdom of someone who was credible and experienced was a powerful moment for me; I had read about Xavier's success rates, but it was another thing to talk to someone who

---

6 Historically Black Colleges and Universities. See the U.S. Department of Education: <https://bit.ly/3kvulRf>

was a part of that success. I was then able to let go of the distractions in my head that were drawing me to other schools—schools where I may have landed without a clear conviction about my destiny and the support system Xavier is renowned for. I now had a practical plan I could articulate and a path upon which to set myself. And as it turned out, I soon learned I wasn't alone; I had many friends who were also headed to the Big Easy and Xavier.

Armed with this salient advice, I settled into an upstream journey to become a physician. As the sun set on Granddad's life and the United States flag draped his casket during the funeral, I knew that his spirit would be with me on my journey forward. On that journey, I would also carry with me the hope of my maternal grandfather, a sharecropper born in the nineteenth century to parents who endured slavery, as I pursued education and training that would stretch into the twenty-first century. Every generation had cared for their families and uniquely contributed to their communities, making many sacrifices along the way, and cumulatively their hard work and deep faith had brought me to this point. I knew it was time for me to do my part, rise to the occasion, and fulfill my purpose. My mission would not be about personal achievement but rather a career of service that would improve the health and quality of life for the less fortunate. Through God's grace and mercy, and despite my imperfections, I knew I could become an instrument of His love through healing and advocacy.

CHAPTER 5

Xavier and Brotherhood

Early one hot August morning, my mom and I began the five-hour drive from Shreveport to New Orleans, which marked the beginning of my college years. My mom had rented a hotel room for a night, and we'd made a long list of things I needed to buy that afternoon so I could hit the ground running once I arrived on campus. As with much of southern Louisiana, there's no such thing as a summer day in New Orleans without rain and humidity. My mother was already nervous about leaving me in what she called "sin city," but when a flash flood hit as we were leaving a department store and she needed to briefly navigate the car through two feet of water, the aghast look on her face was priceless. By the time we made it back to the hotel, I think the very last of all of her nerves was frayed.

With all my basic items bought and ready, we arrived on campus the next day for the moving-in process. I met my new roommate, a young man from Texas, and the freshman orientation team helped me move my belongings into St. Michael's Hall. At that time, St. Michael's was the sole dormitory for males on campus, and Xavier didn't have coed dormitories. (As the nation's only historically Black, Catholic university, Xavier was conservative in many ways.) While my alma mater has since built new residence halls, for decades St. Michael's was a staple experience for the young men of Xavier. During the Civil Rights Movement, our beloved St. Mike's secretly housed the Freedom Riders for a week when they couldn't find safe accommodation elsewhere in the city.[7] There was history in the walls of the building.

Freshman orientation was a blast. From pride-generating chants to parties where we learned the dance moves to DJ Jubilee's "Get Ready, Ready!" and "Jubilee All," we created unforgettable memories and forged bonds that would last well beyond college. Our welcome to Xavier was overseen by the young and energetic Kevin Hill, Esq., a Xavier alum who was the director of orientation and new student programs in the Department of Student Services. The Peer Dean Association was run out of his office, and the association's members hailed from all across the nation and came from all walks of life. Like many of my new first-year classmates, the association's students were instrumental in making Xavier my new home. All incoming students like me had the goal of walking across the stage with a degree in four years, and the peer deans helped us understand all we needed to do to be successful and the pitfalls to avoid. To put it plainly, many of these young women and men were the embodiment of our dreams. We admired the peer deans for their experience and status, of course, but on top of that—since Xavier was very proactive about spreading good news—as seniors were accepted into law school, dental school, medical school, pharmacy school, etc., the university would announce their

---

7 The University of New Orleans: <https://bit.ly/3kNyypf>

accomplishments. As freshmen, we saw the names of our peer deans throughout the year; this bolstered the credibility of the wisdom they had imparted to us just before school started.

Of the many pieces of advice the peer deans offered us during orientation, one still stands out to me. We were to expect courses to be challenging, but we should never have too much pride to ask for help; in fact, they encouraged us to go to the tutoring lab even if we felt like we were on top of things, as it was better to discover and resolve our gaps in the lab than on an exam. That first semester, in general chemistry, I almost learned this lesson the hard way, but I sought help and actually did well. Learning was a team effort at Xavier; our aspirations were high, but we shared our knowledge and didn't view each other as competitors. By asking for help in chemistry, I was able to embrace, devoid of pride, a regular study routine that strengthened my GPA while also leaving me time to explore the other facets of campus life.

New Orleans is a historic city with rich traditions that distinguish it from other cities in Louisiana. It's famous for its distinctive music, lively nightlife, festivals and parades, unique dialects, and Creole and Cajun foods; the city reflects a melting-pot of American, French, and West African cultures. I knew this would be an amazing place to go to college, and I was looking forward to Mardi Gras and Jazz Fest in particular. When I first arrived on campus, I was pretty sure that, somewhere in New Orleans, there was a party every night. My suspicion was confirmed as soon as orientation was over and the weekend before classes arrived. My very first college party was the annual Kappa Labor Day celebration at a downtown hotel. Students from everywhere had come back to school, and the grand ballroom was a beautiful oasis. The future doctors, lawyers, educators, business leaders, and scientists of America were in attendance and looking their very best. I was impressed. As on campus, the gentlemen were outnumbered by the intelligent women of Xavier, who partied hard that weekend before we all hit the books the following week.

As a premed student, I joined a large class of Xavier biomedical scholars led by the legendary J.W. Carmichael, who had headed the program since the 1970s. Unlike some of my classmates who had physicians and dentists in their families, I had a lot to learn about the steps to realizing my dream. Some students had completed one of Xavier's summer science programs before freshmen orientation, while others already had their sights set on the next summer's research programs. In some ways, I felt behind before the semester really even started. Yet, within just a matter of weeks, it became clear to me why Xavier's premedical and pre-health program was so renowned: starting from the first week, we were prepped for success. The entire medical-school application-process was demystified, and we were set on a multi-year path to assembling our application package even as we advanced academically. During my first year, we began writing the personal essay portion of our medical school applications, and we took practice Medical College Admission Tests (MCATs) in preparation for the day when we would sit the real exam. Notably, too, the premed office had all manner of tools to help us: back when computers were not ubiquitous and the Internet was still nascent, the premed office had multiple Apple workstations for student use. Each computer was loaded with data on summer research and internship programs as well as with various statistical analyses on the success of Xavier graduates. Researching summer supplemental programs and internships, and later applying to graduate programs, was a data-informed process. I was grateful to be in the right place for success.

I enjoyed the transition to college life. Unlike high school, I wasn't in class all day, so I had time to review material or read ahead in my textbooks before class. (Of course, having the option to sneak in some extra studying is different from *actually* doing it, and there were plenty of afternoons when I enjoyed myself in the Yard—i.e., Xavier's campus quad.) As a biology major, most semesters I had at least two science courses, both with a lecture and a lab.

While the academic rigor of Xavier was formidable, it was not a place where it was easy to fail, as long as you were willing to put in the work; Xavier would extend its network of resources to any student willing to achieve. The student-to-faculty ratio was small, and professors knew you by your first name. You were required to attend classes, and the university had a practice of sending a copy of your grades to your home address so parents or guardians could review your semester-end report. Admittedly not everyone was a fan of this setup, but it contributed to the family-like experience and to the success of the university in preparing its students to help create a more just and humane society. In the premed program specifically—and unlike programs in many other schools—under Dr. Carmichael, it was assumed that we *would* all succeed, and rather than students being pitted against each other in competition, we were encouraged to work together, form student study groups, and support each other. For example, without my classmates, I'm not sure I would've made it through our organic-chemistry drill class. This class was in addition to our chemistry lecture and lab classes, and it seemed like we were continuously quizzed on the construction of our three-dimensional, ball-and-stick models, each of which stood for a chemical compound or molecule, the individual parts of which we were required to know inside and out.

When I arrived at Xavier in 1994, there was no campus fitness center where I could pump iron and stay in shape. We did have student-organized aerobics classes that were held in the Barn (our affectionate name for Xavier's practice sports venue) a few nights each week, and I sometimes availed myself of those. A few of us guys would drop in on the back row; it was quite a scene whenever the house tune "Coffee Pot (It's Time for the Percolator)" played, and we all swung our knees out wildly doing the accompanying dance. Additionally, groups of students jogged around campus some evenings, and for me, there was occasional access to the Gert Town Natatorium just across the canal from campus. As a swimmer, I enjoyed my visits to the pool, especially because this was the first time I'd ever seen an African American swim team. However, the natatorium was aged, and many of us students were looking for a facility that was more modern and had broader workout options.

Not too far from campus was a French Riviera Fitness franchise. Like many Xavier students, I took advantage of a student-discount package the gym was offering and signed up for a trial membership. After working out at the gym a few times and reading the fine print of the membership agreement, I decided to cancel my membership in accordance with the cancellation provision. When I spoke to a staff member at the gym, he was very persuasive and clearly didn't want to let me out of the contract. I was pretty firm, but even still I had to make another trip back to the gym on the last day that I could cancel without penalty. Given the difficulty I had, I suspected other students had been bullied into keeping their memberships, and I believed Xavier could do more to shield students from being taken advantage of. Young, naive, and impatient, like many college students, I wanted to spark change.

Within a matter of days, I sent a letter to Xavier's president, Dr.

Norman C. Francis—a man of such distinction that he would later receive the Presidential Medal of Honor. His executive assistant Karen Watkins received it first. In my letter, I asked if Xavier could set up an arrangement with French Riviera Fitness on behalf of students as an interim measure while developing plans to build a fitness center on campus. My singular goal was to solve a problem, however, I was swimming outside of my lane. At the time, I was not a student leader, nor had I sought the counsel of faculty or staff before penning my note. I suspect that as soon as Ms. Watkins read my letter, she made a few calls to find out more about the impetuous freshman student who—seemingly out of nowhere—had asked Xavier to invest millions into building a campus gym. When I next met Kevin Hill, who probably knew more first-year students than anyone else on campus, he'd clearly spoken with Ms. Watkins. He shot me a particularly special look; it was somewhere between "I hope you know what you're doing," and "Let's be more strategic the next time you want to get something done." I figured that would be the last of it, but to my surprise, I received a response from Dr. Francis in my campus mailbox, and I was invited to call Ms. Watkins to schedule an appointment with him.

On the day of my appointment, I dressed myself nicely in a pair of slacks and a shirt, and I arrived at the president's office early. I waited patiently to be called into the meeting. When we spoke, Dr. Francis was very accessible and engaging; we talked about his team's planning for the growth of the university, and he acknowledged the need for a gym on campus. While a fitness center wasn't a high priority at that time, Dr. Francis did channel my interest in this area by connecting me with Mr. Sean Lewis, the director of Facilities Planning and Management. I became a student-participant in the finishing stages of the newest dormitory on campus, and over time, I was also able to give input into the design for a fitness center. The fitness center wouldn't be built during my college years, but it did, in due time, come to fruition.

My first meeting with Dr. Francis was the beginning of several influential Xavier relationships that would extend well beyond my years as a college student. Notably, too, this was also the start of a lifelong friendship with Ms. Watkins. During my time at Xavier, she helped me navigate the university as a student leader, and she also set the benchmark in my mind for the excellence an executive assistant should espouse. We're still in touch, and she has been a sounding board for me well into my years as a physician-executive. To this day, my first birthday wish each year comes from Ms. Karen Watkins.

Several students from my high-school graduating class had also chosen Xavier, including some kids I had come up with in elementary school. I was lucky that I didn't have to start from scratch socially my first year. That was helpful, but I soon learned that my class schedule (including lecture and lab sessions on Fridays), was not optimal for Xavier's social scene. Every Friday, starting from about noon, the Yard was the place to be until the parties started in the evening or a basketball game tipped off in the Barn. Juniors and seniors knew to schedule their classes around Xavier's Fridays, and their revelry looked good to me.

Wearing their respective colors and sounding off in foreign-sounding calls and chants, sorority members dominated the Yard each week. The ladies of Alpha Kappa Alpha, Delta Sigma Theta, Zeta Phi Beta, and Sigma Gamma Rho lounged on their traditional plots, singing songs and taking pride in their sisterhood. Not to be outdone, the men of Xavier's fraternities made their presence known. Always outnumbered by the ladies, the men of Alpha Phi Alpha, Kappa Alpha Psi, Omega Psi Phi, and Phi Beta Sigma came out in force, representing their various traditions. At about 5:30 p.m., just outside the Student Center, the Xavier Patio Show—informal student performances—would kick off to the music of a DJ; this brought together all of Xavier's students for the first party of the weekend. And of course, no Patio Show would be incomplete without a stroll or two from Xavier's fraternities and sororities, all of which are National Pan Hellenic Council members, as brothers and sisters showed off their latest stepping moves.

As a freshman, this world of Greek fraternities was foreign to me. (I had seen the Spike Lee movie *School Daze*, but it was not fresh in my mind.) But as I watched the Yard each week, my interest in Greek life grew. Xavier students were not eligible for Greek membership until their sophomore year, and my casual conversations with my freshmen friends usually led to our own comparisons and critiques of the fraternities, sororities, and their members. However, by the end of that year, our casual chatter became more hushed as we learned that expressing membership interest in a fraternity or sorority was a discrete process, one that was dictated by unwritten rules that we were figuring out. Yet, even what we thought we knew we did not really know.

~

OF THE FOUR FRATERNITIES ON CAMPUS, KAPPA ALPHA PSI FRATERNIty, Inc. called to me. Affectionately known as the Nupes, these smooth and debonaire brothers had the nicest diamond-shaped plot on the Yard, and it was always meticulously painted in the Kappa colors of crimson and cream. Wearing their aviator sunglasses and twirling their red-and-white-striped canes, the Nupes were the best-dressed young men on campus, and they exuded class and sophistication. Yet Nupes were far more than young men who stepped out at the Patio Show; they were also campus leaders who embodied the Kappa motto, "Achievement in every field of human endeavor."

Kappa men were part of a tradition that was established in 1911 on the campus of Indiana University Bloomington. The founders were men of the same era as my maternal grandfather, but instead of sharecropping, they found themselves on a predominantly white college campus—one that far from welcomed them. Although Indiana University Bloomington admitted Black men as students, it simultaneously denied them the use of campus facilities like dorms and athletic fields. It was under these circumstances that ten young men, seeking confraternity predicated on Black achievement, formed the first Kappa chapter. As I learned more about Kappa history, I gained a sense of how remarkable the founders' personal achievements were compared to their peers, especially in light of the oppression and racism they experienced. Through their struggle, sacrifice, and service to others, they created a fraternity that would eventually stretch its reach to all corners of this nation and beyond. And with every new pledge year, more students pursuing careers in business, education, law, medicine, and dentistry (to name a few), joined the ranks of Kappa Alpha Psi's men.

Pursuing membership in a sorority or fraternity was not easy. It began with the delicate art of expressing your interest with humility while at the same time not being visibly awestruck in the presence of members. For youthful and impressionable students like me, it wasn't difficult to get sucked into seeking the favor of individual sorority or fraternity members through doing benign tasks or submitting to physical hazing.

For potential Kappa Alpha Psi members specifically, in addition to evidencing qualities like maturity and dedication, and on top of holding a minimum GPA of 2.5, a personal letter of interest and several letters of recommendation from community leaders and/or fraternity members were mandatory. From there, if your application advanced to the next round, an in-person interview was also required. Both then and now, joining Kappa Alpha Psi is a lifelong commitment—to the fraternity itself *and* to ongoing personal achievement/excellence—and before the Kappas admit any new member, each candidate must embrace the depth and solemnity of the commitment being made.

I wanted to be a Nupe, but I was intimidated about measuring up since I knew there was more to Kappa membership than what I could see on the outside. The air of mystery forced me to confront the areas in which I needed to grow personally and yet challenged me to step beyond my comfort zone. One of the most serious Kappas I met in the Yard was Kevin Sneed, who was a doctoral candidate in the College of Pharmacy. He knew of my interest in the fraternity, and on one Friday afternoon, his eyes locked on mine as I crossed the Yard. Within seconds, we were face-to-face discussing Kappa life, achievement, and my future development. He understood the art of recruitment and was intentional in his expectations. Like so many others who have supported me in my lifetime, he saw in me what I didn't see in myself at the time, and he wanted me to know that Kappa Alpha Psi was the fraternity where I belonged.

In 1996, in my sophomore year, I was privileged to join the Beta Iota Chapter of Kappa Alpha Psi at Xavier. Twelve pledges strong, my line was the first to cross at the chapter in several years following a national moratorium, and we stood for rebirth. Kevin Hill was our chapter advisor, and his counsel was always wise. As a former Beta Iota initiate, he had lived the Kappa experience at Xavier, and additionally he brought with him the dual perspective of a campus administrator and an attorney. While there was no doubt that neophytes like me would have a good time as members, his focus remained on our future achievements, with a special emphasis on our continuing to graduate school. As we worked through the myriad of decisions in front of us as young, energetic, and naive men, Kevin Hill worked tirelessly to infuse perspective and vision into our aspirations.

From community service to the social scene, we immersed ourselves in fraternal life. Since the facilities on campus couldn't accommodate our parties, it was customary for us to rent out a ballroom at one of the larger New Orleans hotels like the Marriott or Hilton. Once we even hosted a party at the Louisiana Superdome, the largest venue in New Orleans. By collaborating with our older brothers, we learned the business of contracting with venues for fraternity events. Collectively, we raised thousands of dollars to support our chapter operations and service activities, and in 1997, the Beta Iota Chapter was able to donate one thousand dollars—the largest gift to date ever received from an undergraduate chapter—to the Kappa Alpha Psi Foundation.

I enjoyed being a Kappa man at Xavier, and in terms of my service obligations, I was particularly drawn to mentoring. As I advanced and expanded my own dreams, I realized that I could help others do the same. Every chance I got, either with the Kappas or with other campus organizations, I visited local elementary schools where I tutored young students in math and science. While many of the students we engaged with didn't understand what college was all about, they did know the name Xavier; our visits put smiles on their faces, and I'd like to think we inspired at least a few of them to strive for a college education.

Another element of my service was my involvement in the "Kappa's Klothes for Kids" initiative. As college students, we understood that young people cared about their clothes and appearance, but we also knew that many of the children we worked with came from households that were struggling financially. In 1997, our chapter decided on a clothing drive, and I came up with the idea of partnering with Russell's Cleaners, a local dry cleaner that I had used occasionally, to support our effort. We worked with Russell's to encourage their patrons and other members of the community to donate clothes at one of their three locations, and Russell's cleaned the clothes for free.

When I first joined the Kappas, beyond getting a handle on campus/local activities, I had a lot to learn about the fraternity on the regional and national levels. Within months of becoming a member, my new brothers and I attended our first regional Kappa conference, which was held in my hometown of Shreveport. In the weeks leading up to the conference, some chapter advisors and alumni members, citing my discipline, encouraged me to run for strategus of the Southwestern Province, an office equivalent to a sergeant-at-arms. (My being elected to this office would allow our chapter and our state of Louisiana to have undergraduate representation at the leadership level, and to this day I suspect Kevin Hill was one of the men who put my name forward for the position.) I didn't really understand what the process would entail, but I trusted the guidance of our Kappa elders and put my best foot forward. Once I made the commitment, my brothers ensured I had the support I needed; Irving Johnson, III did a photo shoot with me in his campus studio, and from there he helped me design my campaign flyer. At the regional conference, my line brothers distributed that flyer across the various meetings, ensuring that everyone in attendance knew of my candidacy. It was there at the conference that I was introduced to the caucus structure, and a seasoned Dr. Wallace Davenport, a vice-chancellor at Southern University, took me under his wing. He shepherded me from caucus to caucus, and again and again I gave my campaign speech in the hopes of convincing delegates to vote for me. Looking back, it really wasn't a competitive race and I easily won, but I learned a lot by running for office. Strategus was a lower-level position, but now I would be in the room where the action happened.

My job as strategus was a humble enough one—for the most part, I simply guarded the door during our province meetings. (These meetings were held in various locations across the Southwestern Province's five states.) Yet at the same time, I saw the embodiment of the Kappa motto in those rooms. United in their love for and service to the fraternity, alumni officers were seasoned professionals from a variety of professions. Until the first time I guarded the meeting-room door, I had never been in a room with a cadre of such highly accomplished Black and African American men. As my service continued, I learned how to run a meeting according to Robert's Rules of Order, and I came to understand the inner politics of the organization. Specifically, I remember marveling at the crisp presentations given by Mr. Rhen C. Bass, a sharp certified public accountant who never minced his words.

Although my role of strategus counted as service to the fraternity, I received far more than I gave. I wasn't treated like a fly on the wall; these men embraced me and believed that I had more to offer. Of the many men who supported me, none were more influential than our regional president, Dwayne M. Murray, Esq., who believed in training younger members for leadership. As he lived just an hour away in Baton Rouge, we quickly developed a close relationship. He progressively assigned tasks to me beyond my initial duties to both evaluate me and prepare me for the future. (Given that our region was home to more chapters than anywhere else in the nation, there was plenty of work to go around.) The following year, he encouraged me to run for the undergraduate regional vice president. By then I understood the process of running, but a regional position wasn't a goal I had established for myself. However, the regional board *also* wanted me to run, and with so many of my brothers encouraging me to step up and recruiting me for the role, I was introduced to the notion of leaders being called to serve.

Although I had never personally set my sights on the vice presidency, I was more than prepared for the position. I understood the issues facing the fraternity well, and I had developed name recognition and credibility with many delegates. I won the election and, late in my junior year, I began a one-year term as a regional leader of fifty-five undergraduate chapters across our five-state region. Almost immediately, any issue related to the concerns or needs of our chapters was sent to me to manage, and often I worked with members of the board to address challenging issues. I also had the privilege of visiting other campuses and being invited to speak at—or otherwise participate in—programs for both undergraduate and alumni chapters.

Assuming leadership positions was not easy as an undergraduate, but it led to tremendous personal growth that better prepared me for the obstacles of life down the road. The local-, regional-, and national-level relationships I forged back then remain strong to this day. Looking back at some of the exceptional men who fostered me is, even now, still inspiring; two of them, Dwayne M. Murray, Esq. and W. Randy Bates,

Esq., would later become national presidents of the fraternity, and a third—Rhen C. Bass—would become the fraternity's national treasurer-secretary. Our local New Orleans alumni chapter president Dr. Romell Madison, also a mentor of mine, would go on to serve as president of the National Dental Association. These men, and many more like them, shared their triumphs, defeats, and wisdom with young men like me, providing counsel that would shape us. The benefit of their collective experience could not be qualified.

CHAPTER 6

The Journey from College to Medical School

As my senior year at Xavier raced forward, I began to feel the pressure of a dream possibly deferred. Like many of my friends, I'd applied strategically to medical schools across the nation. While my grades were pretty good, and my leadership and extracurriculars were stellar, I didn't prepare well for the *Medical College Admission Test* (MCAT), and I didn't score competitively. Like many medical-school hopefuls, I had enrolled in a Kaplan MCAT review course, but looking back, I know that I didn't optimally apply all that I'd learned to the exam. A non-competitive score was a sizeable flaw in my medical-school application package, but I decided to move forward with the application process, nonetheless. If I were unsuccessful in placing at a school, I would have to take the exam again before reapplying the following year.

I could only hope my letters of recommendation would mitigate my MCAT deficiency. I had letters from three strong voices. One was from Xavier's president Dr. Norman C. Francis, who I'd grown to know well because of my student leadership. A second came from

Dr. Deidre Labat, Dean of the College of Arts and Sciences; she was a professor of mine and a faculty advisor to those of us on the University Planning Council. The third was penned by Dr. Michelle Bell Boissiere, my biology professor and direct advisor. Having these three influential voices behind me helped quell my uncertainty, although I still really wasn't sure where I stood; I knew MCAT scores were a key component of any medical-school application package and were frequently used to determine which applicants would be invited to campus for an interview.

The waiting game began. Days and weeks passed by with few answers. To boost my chances of being offered an interview, I also sent, whenever possible, secondary applications—i.e., much more personal appeals to schools—to make the case that I was a good candidate and should be granted an interview. By late fall, I began to receive responses in the mail, and I quickly realized that a thin envelope was not a good sign. School after school thanked me for applying and encouraged me to try again next year, and this included every medical school in my home state of Louisiana.

This was a challenging period for me. Again and again, I recalled that Xavier consistently places more Black and African American students in medical schools each year than any other university in the nation. There was no better place to be for someone with my background and dreams. If I couldn't be successful here, what would that mean? After all, it was this very scenario—the prospect of failure and not being accepted to medical school—that had fueled my initial hesitancy about declaring my dream of becoming a physician before college. Now, as rejection letters poured in, I was facing this potential reality and feeling as if my future and the hopes and dreams of those who believed in me were at stake. I found myself at a crossroads that tested my determination, my faith, and the desire of my heart.

Waiting around without action was not the thing for a Xavier student to do, so I decided to make alternate plans. From November to January, I applied to several osteopathic medical schools to broaden my options. (Allopathic applications and osteopathic applications are two separate processes.) My first breakthrough was when I was invited to interview at the College of Osteopathic Medicine at Western University of Health Sciences in California. I flew out to Los Angeles and stayed at the home of my uncle James in Watts, a neighborhood in South Central. He let me drive his manual, Nissan truck to Pomona for my interview. This was back before GPS was widely available; I followed his hand-written directions as I shifted the gears of the truck through Los Angeles County's heavy, stop-and-go traffic until I arrived (on time) on campus. As with most medical-school interviews, mine wasn't merely one meeting, rather it was a daylong event of various tours and presentations. I enjoyed the day on campus, met a few Xavier graduates who were enrolled and prospering at Western, and found myself excited by the opportunities at Western and the prospect of living in California.

Not long afterward, I was granted an interview at the College of Medicine at Howard University in Washington, DC. A fellow Xavier student arranged for me to stay with her parents, and when I arrived in DC, they greeted me with hospitality and even drove me to and from my interview. I also carried with me Dr. Francis' sage advice: "Xavier will get you a ticket to the dance, but once you get there, *you* have to do the dancing." I heeded his words. From my crisp black suit to the firmness of my handshakes and consistent eye contact with those I met,

I put forward my best effort all day. Walking through the halls of Howard's College of Medicine reminded me of my strolls along the huge levees of the Mississippi River behind my apartment in New Orleans: I saw a legacy of success at Howard that was as vast as the breadth of the river. Howard presented the chance for me to stand on the huge shoulders of the more than one-hundred-and-twenty-five classes of graduates whose photos hung on the walls. It was truly an impressive day of meeting the students and faculty of the College of Medicine, and after discussions with those I met, I was confident that I could thrive at Howard and further my dream of becoming a physician.

One of the lessons we were taught in Dr. Carmichael's premed program at Xavier was this: your medical-school interview starts the moment you step foot on campus and doesn't end until you leave. During my interview day at Howard, I learned first-hand just how true this was. At the end of the day, hoping to touch base with a mentor and friend, I called Dr. Antoine Garibaldi to see if I could stop by his office. Dr. Garibaldi had been vice president of Academic Affairs at Xavier when I was a first-year student, but he'd left the school to become Howard's first provost and chief academic officer. Dr. Garibaldi (who today is president of the University of Detroit Mercy) is an exceptional educator and leader; when I knew him at Xavier, he made it his business to memorize the names of students and greet us individually, and he made us all feel valued. To this day, he is still a walking encyclopedia of information about the students and faculty he's encountered during his career.

Dr. Garibaldi graciously invited me to his office. It was getting dark that early evening as I, still in my suit and oversized trench coat, made the hike up a steep hill toward Howard's main administrative building. By the time I reached his office, I was ready to exhale and relax a bit after a long, demanding day of presenting my very best. Yet when Dr. Garibaldi ushered me in, I was surprised to see a distinguished-looking gentleman seated on the sofa. He had a cool first name and a French last name—Dr. Floyd J. Malveaux. In the next moment, I learned that Dr. Malveaux was the dean of the College of Medicine and vice provost for Health Affairs.

Immediately, I snapped back into full interview mode, eager to make my pitch for becoming part of Howard University and its legacy. As we talked, Dr. Malveaux shared with me a brief overview of his journey from his hometown of Opelousas, LA (a small city about twenty-five miles north of Lafayette) to a career as a researcher, educator, and nationally renowned allergist and immunologist. He himself was a Howard College of Medicine alum, although he hadn't taken the usual route to his degree; *after* earning his PhD from Michigan State University, and *after* taking an instructor's position at Howard, he *then* enrolled himself at Howard and earned his MD.

I was awestruck by Dr. Malveaux's accomplishments, but at the same time I was somewhat shaken. On the one hand, I saw someone who looked like me and shared my Louisiana roots, which inspired me. Yet, on the other hand, his achievements really raised the bar in my mind, and I wasn't sure that my potential would impress him. Nevertheless, I was glad I'd made the call for a quick visit to Dr. Garibaldi's office, and I was deeply appreciative of the effort he'd made in introducing me to Dr. Malveaux. I was now certain that Howard was the school for me, but only time would tell whether I would be accepted into this prestigious institution.

Back on campus at Xavier, I waited and tried to stay busy. A month or so later, a letter from Meharry Medical College in Nashville arrived and notified me that my application package put me in their acceptance range and that I might be granted an interview. This was certainly better than a rejection letter, but I still felt like all my eggs were in one or two baskets; not having many viable options stood in stark contrast to my experience when applying to colleges. Even still, I was grateful for Meharry's consideration. A few months earlier, I had contacted Dr. E.E. Allen, a legendary Shreveport dentist who, in 1970, became the first African American elected official in my hometown since Reconstruction[8] for assistance in gaining an interview at Meharry. He was a 1945 graduate of Meharry's School of Dentistry and the twenty-first grand polemarch (i.e., national president) of Kappa Alpha Psi; he wrote a letter to the dean of the medical school on my behalf in January. Yet time was not my friend at this point. I knew I had learned many valuable lessons outside of the classroom that would someday enrich me as a doctor, but the jury was still out on whether the hard work and study of my undergraduate years would pay off.

As I'd made my way through my undergraduate years, I'd had the chance to meet many exemplary men through Kappa Alpha Psi. Many of them were luminaries on the national stage, such as the famous attorney Johnnie Cochran (also a native of Shreveport, LA), astronaut Dr. Bernard Harris, Congressmen Bennie Thompson and John Conyers, and others. I had kept ongoing correspondences with many of these Kappa alumni, and during my last semester of college, I leaned in for support and guidance from this network. I especially remember letters from Dr. Henry W. Foster Jr., a former dean at Meharry who

---

8 EPDF.Pub: <https://bit.ly/3OPU1eY>

was President Clinton's senior advisor for teen pregnancy reduction and youth issues. His engagement over the years was always encouraging, never more so than in March 1998 as I awaited decisions from schools. Likewise, Percy E. Sutton, a civil rights attorney who represented Malcolm X, kept in touch with me. I was always excited to receive his letters, all of which arrived in distinguished blue envelopes on his personal stationery or on letterhead from his company, the Inner City Broadcasting Corporation. He encouraged me in his March 23, 1998, letter: "If medical school is your dream, <u>follow that dream and never give up.</u>" (Underlining as in original.)

On April 15, 1998, I finally received some positive news in the mail. A letter dated April 6, 1998, said in part, "The Committee on Admissions is pleased to inform you that you have been accepted for admission to the Howard University College of Medicine as a member of the class entering in August 1998." However, there were a number of conditions to my admission, the biggest being my successful completion of Howard's Preliminary Academic Reinforcement Program (PARP), a six-week summer program for incoming medical students. I wasn't sure how to receive this conditional acceptance, but I was committed to moving forward. I immediately filled out the necessary forms for Howard and PARP, and I mailed them off along with my good faith deposit and enrollment fee. Toward the end of April, I was informed that I'd also been accepted to Western University, but I was firmly Howard bound.

On Mother's Day weekend, my Xavier graduation day arrived. My mom and dad joined me in New Orleans that weekend, and many of my mentors and friends attended the ceremony. Like my fraternity brothers, I wore a crimson-and-cream stole over my graduation gown. During an honors and awards presentation that preceded the main ceremony, to my surprise, I received the Saint Katharine Drexel Award, the university's highest student service award, which is named after Xavier's beloved foundress. It was presented to me by Dr. Francis, and it was humbling to share this honor through hugs and photos with many of the people who'd believed in me and the value of my contributions. More importantly, receiving the Drexel Award set my sights high for a lifetime of service.

I returned to Shreveport and was home for just a few weeks before I headed to DC for the PARP summer program. Supported by a grant from the Health Careers Opportunity Program, PARP ran from early June to mid-July and immersed participants in the rigors of first-semester medical-school courses. PARP classes were taught by Howard professors and upper-class people in the medical college, and they gave us a window into the discipline and focus that were needed for the pursuit of a degree in medicine. My class was eighteen students strong, and although we were a diverse group, we were unified by a common commitment to success. We were housed on campus in one dorm building, and we bonded quickly even as we got down to work.

During these summer weeks, I had to face my fears and cherish the opportunity to succeed that I'd been given. PARP was essentially a proving ground for me; my acceptance to Howard was conditional on completing this coursework, and a little voice in the back of my head never let me forget this singular fact. The material we were given was challenging, and I began to stretch the ability of my brain as I learned to consume, process, and retain large volumes of information. I was fortunate in that I'd been paired with an older roommate, Matthew Nelson, who'd had a career in education; he assisted me with study tips and tools, and—just by setting a solid example and sharing his life experience—he helped me mature my thinking. In particular, he made me understand the difference between being familiar with information and truly knowing the material. He also helped me keep the big picture in mind; while it was tempting at times to join some of my peers in lamenting the volume of work, Matthew would quickly steer me into a focused zone where I could use my precious time wisely. With the techniques he shared with me, I successfully completed exam after exam, with my confidence growing stronger and stronger. I knew that I wouldn't have to return home with my mission incomplete.

It was during PARP that I fell in love with whiteboards and dry-erase markers. Although we spent most of our days in class, my classmates and I camped out in our dorm's study rooms each evening and over the weekends. By using whiteboards, I was able to master the details of glycolysis or the Krebs cycle; I would repeatedly write out, in various colors, every step and reaction of a process, then go over the material again and again with my classmates until I memorized it. (I found color coding to be such an effective visual aid that, when a whiteboard wasn't available, I used gel pens in assorted colors to sketch out information and organize it for easy recall and application.) Thanks to my time in PARP, I found a learning tool that worked well for me, one that would help me all through medical school and beyond.

Working with my PARP peers was fantastic. We challenged each other to achieve, shared best practices, and carried each other across the finish line. We all completed the program and successfully entered Howard in August. I started the semester with renewed confidence and few doubts. Although I would soon find that PARP's six weeks only covered the first *week* of medical school's coursework, the supplemental summer course proved to be exactly what I needed to start my medical-school years strong. I'd been taught how to prepare for exams and the power of effective study groups, and the relationships I formed will last a lifetime.

In my earlier years, time and time again, I tried to control my destiny and create the certainty that successful people appear to have. Maturity has taught me that the plan God has is better, even when I don't understand the journey initially. While I originally viewed PARP as a hurdle to medical school, the program instead turned out to be my *key* to success.

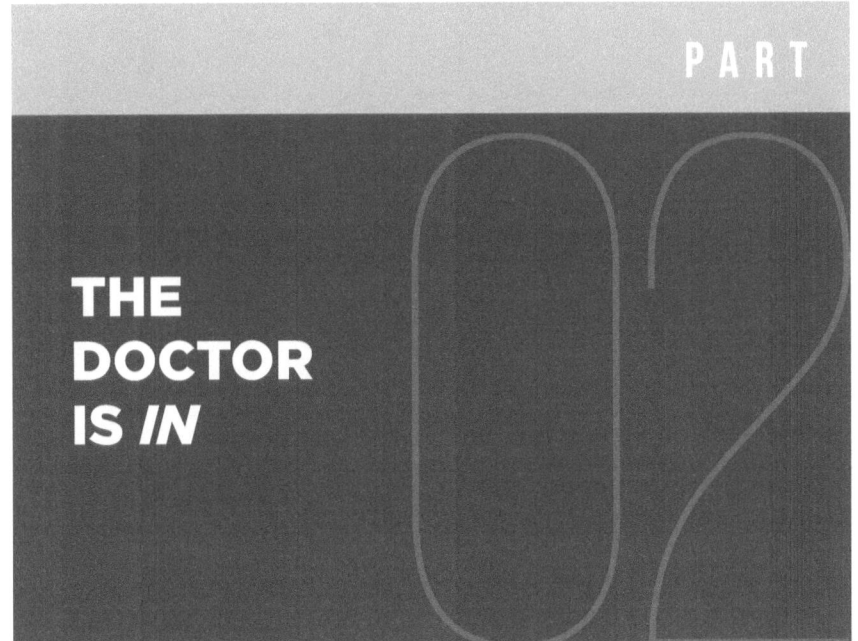

PART

02

THE
DOCTOR
IS *IN*

CHAPTER 7

The First Two Years of Medical School

WHEN THE FALL 1998 SEMESTER BEGAN, I BECAME PART OF HOWARD University's legacy. Founded in 1867 when America was still reeling from the Civil War, Howard was among the first in the nation to accept Black and African American medical students, and in the early twentieth century, it became one of only two historically Black medical schools (Meharry being the other) to survive the aftermath of the 1910 Flexner report.[9] Today, with the addition of Charles R. Drew University and the Morehouse School of Medicine, both of which were established in the mid-twentieth-century, Howard is one of only four HBCU medical schools in the nation. Known as "The Mecca,"

---

9 Abraham Flexner, after being commissioned by the Carnegie Foundation, examined the educational practices of one-hundred-and-fifty-five medical schools in the US and Canada. In his eponymous 1910 report, he proposed the "development of the requisite number of properly supported institutions, and the speedy demise of all others." In the wave of closures that followed, five (of seven) US Black medical schools were shuttered, including the successful Leonard Medical School of Shaw Univ. in Raleigh, NC. Among other troubling statements in his report, Flexner wrote, "The Negro needs good schools rather than many schools." See the National Institutes of Health: <https://bit. ly/3F6WKw7>.

Howard has consistently been a leader in producing America's Black professionals, including those in medicine, pharmacy, dentistry, and nursing. Many pioneering and elite doctors of African descent earned their MDs at Howard, including Dr. Debra Holly Ford (first African American woman to be board-certified in colorectal surgery *and* to become a Fellow of the American College of Colon and Rectal Surgeons); the late Dr. LaSalle D. Leffall, Jr. (First African American president of *both* the American Cancer Society and the American College of Surgeons); and the late Dr. Alyce Gullattee (director of Howard's Institute on Substance Abuse and Addiction and member of White House committees for presidents Nixon, Ford, and Carter). These giants in medicine ensured students like me developed an understanding of Howard's history and, more importantly, they weren't shy about voicing the high expectations they had for our future contributions to medicine and society. As I entered the lecture hall on the first day of classes, the torch was passed to me, and I officially became a member of this new family.

Settling into a routine at the beginning of medical school wasn't too difficult as I had a game plan and a small network. Starting on day one, I scoped out the seating arrangements in the lecture halls, and I quickly grew close to a crew of students on whom I could depend. These were the people I could count on if my pen ran out of ink or if I missed a finer point or two of the professor's while furiously scribbling notes. My first semester started with the basics: biochemistry, gross anatomy, introduction to patient care, and introduction to psychiatry. (While these basics are taught in a more integrated way today, they were discrete subjects when I was in school.) Together, these classes and their content were so demanding that they often consumed every waking hour and minute of the day.

Despite the intensity of my first-semester curriculum, I always looked forward to psychiatry lectures from Dr. Gullattee. She herself was an institution within the field; her treatment was built upon the (then-radical) premise of humility and empathy being essential to the practice, and she planted seeds of advocacy in us all. Among her many other accolades, she was the founder and first president of the Student National Medical Association, the first student organization for under-represented minorities in medicine. Her firebrand authenticity, distinctive headwraps, and white coat adorned with political and/or social justice pins-showed that we could each proudly bring our own uniqueness to physicianship while also reminding us that we had an obligation to better the lives of others, whether at the bedside or beyond.

With professors like Dr. Gullattee supporting me, my cultural transition from Xavier to Howard was pretty smooth. Both institutions placed a high value on teamwork and collaboration, and their overall approach to higher education was similar. As I got to know my classmates better, many of whom had been undergraduate students at large-scale universities and Ivy-League schools, I learned that competition had typically ruled the day in their premed programs. This was in stark contrast to Xavier, where we'd always striven to lift each other up. In fact, when I spoke with my Xavier friends who'd moved on to other medical schools, they confirmed that exclusion and unhealthy competition created a heavy burden on top of medical school's many other stressors. Many of my friends told me their professors *expected* high student-attrition rates, and this belief informed their educational approach. Howard couldn't have been more different. Our faculty wanted us *all* to have successful careers in healthcare, and they actively prepared us for working in an industry that has a long history of excluding physicians of color and even purposefully damaging their careers.[10] Preparing us to work in a world where we weren't especially welcomed meant, among other things, imbedding habits in our learning culture that supported a communal approach to success.

Group study, especially at exam time, was an important part of the learning process as I could test for gaps in my knowledge by talking with my peers and reconciling our notes. There were plenty of times when I missed important points of information and was saved by a classmate who had taken better notes. Exam prep was grueling and bore little resemblance to my test-prep procedures at Xavier. Not only was the volume of information we now needed to know enormous, but as an undergraduate, I had sometimes glossed over more-minor details—not every bit of minutia appeared on our exams. My new classmates disabused me of this understanding and pushed me to master the material, and we routinely left no crumb of information on the table.

When I first moved to DC, I'd rented a two-level town house that was a five-minute drive from campus. (This was the 90s when housing was still relatively cheap, and I got a good deal on my long-term lease.) Since I didn't have the expense of commuting in and out of DC each day, I was able to afford parking in the garage of Howard University Hospital (HUH). Most days, I would sprint home at lunchtime between classes to take a mental break. Even if I was only home for thirty minutes, this allowed me to break up my day and recharge for afternoon classes and study groups. To create the optimal learning envi-

---

10 ProPublica: <https://bit.ly/3vYPRsw>

ronment for me, I used the town house's second bedroom as an office. I hung whiteboards on one side of the room and set up my desk and computer on the other. I had a process for studying that ensured I went over material multiple times: I would copy content from my notebook to my whiteboard, then recopy and color code it in my sketchbook, then lastly I would write key points on flashcards to use later in study groups when exam time rolled around. For the most part, this process worked, and I could always revisit the color-coded information if I needed to. When the audio-file sharing service Napster launched, I used this early version of the platform, with its seemingly unlimited access to music and artists, to create large playlists of my favorite jams to help ward off the monotony of hours upon hours of study.

A crucial tool for group study was reviewing test questions on exams from past years, and I was incredibly fortunate to be granted access to these old tests. One of my fraternity brothers, Melvin Jackson, had a twin sister named Melanie who was a third-year medical student when I started at Howard; she made sure that her mentee Darryl Reese (who was then a second-year medical student) became my mentor. With the two of them in my corner, when school first started, I'd received boxes and boxes of old exams with multiple versions of each, the value of which I would only come to appreciate much later. Using old exams for study was a Howard tradition, and although the questions were never identical on our "live" exams, reading through old tests and getting a sense of their structure and depth was invaluable. Additionally, we also used an educational book series called PreTest; these books were essentially question banks that helped us test our knowledge and understanding of the material in any given course.

Medical students typically had three exams per class over the course of each semester, each administered at roughly the same time, and we usually took five courses per semester. Scores were calculated on a curve, and students received an honors, satisfactory, or unsatisfactory on each test. The ritual of checking exam scores was often filled with equal parts anxiety and excitement. Usually, the day after an exam, someone would send out an email telling us that the scores had been posted. A printout tacked to the wall was sorted by student ID number, and especially in the first few minutes after posting, frenzied students gathered around to see how they scored; I always earned an honors or satisfactory mark. With each exam, I wish I'd held on to my rejection letters from medical schools that hadn't believed I would make a good physician, as I was now well on my way to achieving my dream. Every score confirmed what I knew in my heart: I was in the place that I was supposed to be and receiving a world-class education in our nation's capital.

Like in college, I found some of my classes to be more interesting than others, and gross anatomy was by far my favorite course of the first year. While all of our professors were excellent, it was Dr. Mohammed Ashraf Aziz who had a talent for captivating his students and magically infusing his voice into our thoughts. Whether he was speaking on the path of a nerve, a blood vessel's travel through the body, or the function of an obscure muscle, his lessons certainly stuck with me. Additionally, there was no substitute for spending time with my tank mates (i.e., micro study groups) in the gross anatomy lab where we explored cadavers under Dr. Aziz's wise direction. In the classroom we studied the anatomical drawings in our textbooks, but in the lab, we could examine human bodies and see the variations from body to body, which prepared us for exam time and served as a precursor to clinical practice. I was so enthralled by gross anatomy that during my second year, I jumped at the chance to tutor first-year students in the subject.

The second semester of medical school brought more volume and complexity. While anatomy and an introduction to patient care continued, other classes were replaced with microbiology, immunology, neuroscience, and physiology. This meant I took a six-class course load instead of the usual five. Learning was both fascinating and agonizing because each day was like drinking water from a firehose: every drop of assigned content was foundational and important, and it always came at us at full blast. Downtime to let information soak in virtually didn't exist since the next day always brought an equal (if not greater) amount of information to learn.

Time was a precious commodity that was always fleeting. Not even the weekends brought much relief; Saturday and Sunday were mostly for stitching together the learnings of the week and previewing the next week's content. Perhaps my only true refuge from the demands of school came during Sunday services, when I could be renewed spiritually and reground myself in God's purpose for my life. My cousin, the late Jowava Leggett, Ph.D., who'd been essential to my settling into DC, invited me to adopt her church home, the historic Shiloh Baptist Church, as my own. Church refreshed my soul, and it also gave me the chance to interact, on an entirely different level, with several medical college professors who were members. Beyond that, Shiloh Baptist gave me yet another gift, as I forged lifelong friendships with several congregation members.

When I reflect on physiology and neuroscience during my second semester, the distinctive, deep voice of a professor with a Jamaican accent comes to mind. Dr. C. Ovid Trouth, Sr., who would later go on to author the candid, *Times Are Changing and the Struggle Contin-*

ues, was good friends with one of my fraternity advisors at Xavier, Mr. Green, and when I'd left for Howard, he'd advised me to connect with Dr. Trouth. (Many years before, during Mr. Green's military career, he'd met Dr. Trouth in Germany, and they became good friends.) Dr. Trouth, who passed away in January 2022, was not only a great professor and scientist, but his perspective was deeply informed by his international experience, which I found fascinating and instructive. While neither physiology nor neuroscience was a walk in the park, I was extra motivated to step up my game in these subjects so that all reports back to Mr. Green reflected achievement. On this, I did not disappoint, and when I began my clinical rotations in my third year, I had Dr. Trouth's wife, Dr. Annapurni Jayam-Trouth, as my neurology attending on my first rotation.

Once my first year of school came to an end, I felt as if I'd learned more in a single year than in my entire four in college. I welcomed the summer respite, and I used some of my time off to explore DC's many free museums and sites. But before I knew it, I was back in the classroom. As a second-year student, I was getting closer to the reason I'd enrolled in medical school: to take care of patients. But to do so effectively, I needed to learn the difference between normal and abnormal presentations in patients. Much of my first year had been centered on the body in its normal state of function, but my second year would be a deep immersion into the many things that can go wrong with the human body, along with an introduction to treatments. In microbiology I studied scores of infections from the common to the obscure, and in pharmacology, pathology, genetics, and physiology we examined diseases/abnormalities in much the same way. It was a roller-coaster ride. On some days, I felt like I knew enough about a condition to lend broad medical advice to family and friends, while on other days a quasi-hypochondria loomed, and I wondered if I had some of the conditions we were studying.

Of course, the volume of information to absorb didn't get easier in the second year. During this time, the medical college's classrooms were being modernized with smart technology, and we were relocated to another large lecture hall for most of the year. The late nineties were a transition period across the technological spectrum, and while most professors already used Microsoft PowerPoint for presentations and were eager to teach in smart classrooms, one pathology instructor clung to her projector and thirty-five-millimeter slides. I dreaded the sight of her walking down the lecture hall's long staircase with her slide-carousels in hand; if she carried two or three carousels, this meant a marathon of perhaps two-hundred slides, click after click after click. In the few moments before she started her lecture, I would force myself to move past the fear of the amount of work ahead and set my mind into a more positive state. After all, gross anatomy and pathology overlapped to a degree, as pathology examined the root causes of the many abnormal presentations we'd observed in the anatomy lab. I used my passion for anatomy to inform my approach to pathology, and this put me into a state more receptive to learning—no matter how many slides we reviewed on any given day.

Although pathology can be a gloomy topic, I did have a path-lab professor, Dr. Wilbur F. Jackson, who placed his unique brand of teaching on the subject. Whether he was describing the characteristics of a fatty liver (common) or a hydatidiform mole (rare), he taught in a way that was engaging and unforgettable. Dr. Jackson was clearly old enough to be retired, but he loved to teach, and he donned his trademark bow tie every day. He even produced a pathology series on VHS tape, set to ragtime soundtracks, to summarize the key points that he taught across the year. As a tribute to his excellence, I still have a copy of the series.

With classes rolling along and some basic medical knowledge under my belt, I was eager to find a practicing physician to shadow so I could better connect the dots between my in-the-classroom coursework and real-world clinical care. By using model patients from HUH's family-practice clinic, my introduction to patient care course did cover the basics of giving a standard physical exam, but I itched for something more. To my good fortune, Dr. Ingrid Labat, a Xavier alum, provided me the chance to scratch that itch. She was completing her residency in emergency medicine (EM) at HUH, and she welcomed me whenever she was in the ER. (Ingrid was an older sister of my friend Marc, who was also a Xavier alum, and I knew their parents as well since they too were connected to Xavier.) Dr. Labat was an example of the light at the end of my medical-school tunnel, and—although I must admit I wasn't immediately drawn to EM—I enjoyed hanging out with her during her shifts. Dr. Labat was always happy to see me because she said I was her good luck charm who guaranteed a quiet night in the ER.

The emergency department (ED) at HUH was filled with unique smells, strange instruments, monitors of all sorts, and medical supplies to meet almost any situation. The ER served a wide range of people in need of care, from the acutely ill or injured to those who were high or intoxicated and muttered to themselves in the hallways. The department was a busy ecosystem with healthcare workers playing many various roles, from doctors to orderlies, and the staff knew how to come together and create a symphony like musicians in an orchestra. Of course, whenever I had a chance to shadow Dr. Labat, I was constantly waiting on a high-drama crisis moment to arise, just like I'd seen on TV. Well, this did not occur during those visits. Instead, I watched as she managed patients with congestive heart failure, pneumonia, and abdominal pain (etc.) as I lapped up every bit of information I could.

Fingers and broken glass are a bad combination. One of Dr. Labat's patients was a woman who'd cut her finger while picking up a shattered glass in her kitchen, and her ER visit was the first time I observed a laceration repair. Dr. Labat comforted the patient, numbed and cleaned out the wound, and inspected the laceration as the patient moved her finger as instructed. Dr. Labat taught me about the dangers of missing even a single shard of embedded glass and about using X-rays to find hidden slivers that the naked eye can't detect easily. Since anatomy was fresh in my mind that evening, she reviewed with me which tendons in the finger could be injured by a deep cut and how to test for such an injury. When the patient returned from her X-rays, excitement ran through me when Dr. Labat asked for my help. My job was to keep the field clear by dabbing away the blood created by the suturing needle as Dr. Labat closed the wound; I also got to cut the string of each suture after it was placed, leaving it neither too long nor too short.

During the summer following my second year of medical school, I was thankful to have some time off, but I also knew I needed to actively be preparing for my future. In the last months of the academic year, I'd learned about a variety of research opportunities, most of which would've required me to relocate for the summer. Thankfully, I landed a summer-research spot at the National Institutes of Health in neighboring Bethesda, just over Maryland's state line. The NIH, the nation's leading medical research agency, is situated on a three-hundred-acre campus with twenty-seven institutes and centers. I spent most of my NIH experience in the National Institute of Diabetes and Digestive and Kidney Diseases, where, under a preceptor, I assisted a small group of graduate students with their research on diabetes. It was a top-notch place to spend the summer, and the presence of other Howard medical students certainly made me feel at home. Many Howard College of Medicine faculty were affiliated with NIH, including my pathology professor Dr. Vivian W. Pinn, who was the inaugural full-time director of the NIH's Office of Research on Women's Health. The learning environment was incredible as researchers were working to solve some of the most challenging medical issues of the day, and patients, who enrolled in various trials, traveled from all over the country for treatment from NIH care teams. Even though my research was my main task, I was exposed to many medical conditions I might've otherwise only read about in textbooks, and it was always a privilege when patients shared their lived experiences with me. The weeks seemed to fly by, and the eight-week position culminated in a day of poster-presentations from all of us in the summer program.

Every day I spent at NIH helped me grow my knowledge base, and just as importantly, by completing the program I had gained credible research experience that would make me more attractive to residency training-programs later on. I didn't have a true career model or specialty interest in mind quite yet, although I was leaning toward becoming a family physician so I could provide care for patients from birth to end-of-life. As a rising third-year student, I still had some time left to contemplate the direction I wanted to pursue for my residency. It wasn't until my clinical years of medical school that I began to hear the calling of the specialty of my destiny.

CHAPTER 8

The Clinical Years of Medical School: With the Finish Line in Sight

AT MEDICAL SCHOOLS IN THE US AND CANADA, STUDENTS SPEND THEIR first two years in the classroom, then, upon passing the first of three exams leading to licensure,[11] they advance to clerkships in teaching hospitals. Third- and fourth-year students are considered acting interns and are closely overseen by both residents and attendings. For Howard College of Medicine students, entering the third year meant crossing the connecting bridge between the Seeley G. Mudd Building's hallowed halls and HUH. With the bridge crossed, we would then spend the next two years rotating through seven core specialties—internal medicine, surgery, pediatrics, psychiatry, neurology and rehabilitation, obstetrics and gynecology, and family medicine—as well as several elective specialties.

---

11 The United States Medical Licensing Examination Step 1, a seven-part daylong test, assesses a medical student's ability to apply scientific concepts to the practice of medicine. Earning a highly competitive score on Step 1 was traditionally considered among the most-weighted factors of a graduating medical student's placement into a residency program. However, per the USMLE's website, as of Jan. 2022, Step 1 became a pass/fail test.

When I reported to HUH on the first day, I felt it was going to be an exciting year; the hard work I'd put into my first two years of school was beginning to pay off, and at long last I felt my goal of becoming a real physician was within reach. Each of my rotations would be in blocks from four to eight weeks, and for the first time I would really get to see the day-in, day-out grind that doctors, no matter their specialty, face every day. Although my white coat was short (which signifies medical-student status), I wore it proudly with my stethoscope draped around my neck. I stuffed the pockets of that coat with index cards, pocket-reference books, and simple diagnostic tools like my reflex hammer and tuning fork. Knowing I would now play an important role in the healing process for patients was exhilarating, but at the same time I had to acknowledge my limitations as a student. Patients would now place their trust in me, and I regarded that trust as a privilege. As I would soon learn, the health and survival of my patients reinvigorated my drive for learning all I could day after day.

For most clerkships, our days began with rounds. Early in the morning, after the prep of pre-rounding, students and residents would gather at the time set by the attending physician. On rounds, we would go from patient to patient as a group. Although students like me mostly observed during rounds, we *were* actively and mercilessly quizzed (which is called *pimping*) on all kinds of information related to patients' clinical courses, diagnoses, potential complications, and treatments. When an attending singled one of us out to answer a question, no one wanted to face the humiliation of freezing up or giving the wrong response; to stay on top of our game at all times, we had to study patient conditions (and other illnesses within the specialty) during non-working hours and often well into the night. Depending on the attending physician and the residents on any given team, rounds could be quite efficient or drag on for hours. Either way, rounding was a grueling, but effective, teaching process that linked textbook learning and clinical application.

When it came time for my family medicine rotation, I was especially excited. Our faculty cared about students as learners, and they took the time to teach us well. Seeing patients in the clinic with my fellow medical students (while under the watchful eyes of attendings and residents), taught me a lot about professionalism, the importance of obtaining a good social history (to understand the life circumstances of a patient), and the necessity of early-detection screening for conditions like cancer. Most days, the clinic's waiting room was full, and there was plenty of need for acting interns like me. Unfortunately, I also found myself losing enthusiasm for the specialty I thought I wanted to pursue. The pace of family medicine was a bit slower than I'd expected, and I didn't enjoy reconciling the long lists of maintenance medications that patients took to manage chronic conditions like high blood pressure, diabetes, or elevated cholesterol levels. One day, when a woman came in with about twenty prescription bottles asking we go through each one, a moment of clarity hit me, and I began thinking I should explore other specialties.

However, I did enjoy some of the patient interactions on this rotation, especially with the older population. One challenging encounter I navigated with a fellow classmate (who is today a neurosurgeon) stands out. An eighty-year-old man dressed in starched, iron-creased khakis, a plaid blazer, and a brown hat that was cocked to one side came into the clinic. He tested positive for both syphilis and HIV, and since he was sexually active, he was very much in need of guidance on safer sex practices. The multigenerational divide during our discussion was apparent as my classmate and I reviewed his sexual history with him and explained the critical importance of using latex condoms to prevent the transmission of his infections. Our attending, who was undoubtedly familiar with the patient and could easily assess the quality of our care for him, was clearly very interested in our approach to this particular case. He watched intensely as we discussed treatment options with the patient. In the end, our attending commended us for our thoroughness and humility, and we could only hope the patient would heed our advice.

My internal medicine rotation was a daily grind within a crucible of illness and advanced disease, but it did teach me a lot about discipline and the responsibility doctors have to their patients. Starting early in the morning, I would be among the first to speak with those inpatients who'd been assigned to me. I would examine them physically, check their lab and imaging results, and develop a draft plan of care that would later be approved (or adjusted) by an attending. I learned how to negotiate with the nurses on the wards to get tasks done efficiently; each nurse seemingly had a job description that depended on who was making the request and how respectfully the request was made. I also learned how to draw blood for lab testing and change out a Foley catheter, among other hands-on essentials.

This clerkship marked the first time I responded to a cardiac arrest. At most hospitals, cardiac arrests are known as "code blues," but at HUH they're called "Dr. Dans" in honor of Dr. Daniel Hale Williams, the first physician to successfully perform open-heart surgery and the only African American charter member of the American College of Surgeons. This evening was my first time on call, and our team of students and residents was responsible for the patients on our service until the next morning. When a nurse saw that a patient's condition was rapidly deteriorating, she pressed the emergency button above his bed. Hearing the Dr. Dan code, I rushed to the room to help with the all-hands-on-deck response. In the next instant, I was giving the patient chest compressions as the anesthesia residents ran into the room; they supported his breathing by emergently placing a tube into his airway as nurses administered medications from the crash cart.

Unfortunately, our efforts to revive the patient were unsuccessful, and my first Dr. Dan became the moment when I lost my first patient, an eventuality I'd always known I would have to face. As the room began to decompress and the nurses turned the monitors off, a stillness crept through the air. I stayed in the room for a little while as a way of paying my respects. I expected a debriefing session to follow, but none came. The seasoned team of professionals who'd responded to the Dr. Dan wore invisible armor around their emotions, and this armor had been readily apparent as they'd tried to save this man. While this battle for continued life had been lost, our mission still remained: caring for others. In time, I too would learn to wear my emotional armor, just as I would learn when to ask for help and share my emotional load with others.

My inpatient pediatric rotation was probably the roughest of the core clerkships in terms of my interests and career aspirations. Caring for children is always a bit trickier than dealing with adults (who can explain their health concerns), and I quickly realized that I needed to step up my skills with kids. I employed distraction techniques to lessen children's fears during examinations or painful procedures like IV placements, and I learned how to reward my young patients for being brave. While the number of patients on our pediatric service was small compared to other rotations, it wasn't uncommon for us to care for children living with sickle cell disease who were in the midst of pain crises. Howard was (and still is) well-regarded for both its research on sickle cell anemia and its tradition of providing empathetic care, but I didn't really enjoy working with the twelve-and-under set. However, I did find both the adolescent clinic and the youth emergency department interesting. Under the supervision of pediatricians like Dr. Renee Jenkins—the first African American president of both the American Academy of Pediatrics *and* the Society of Adolescent Medicine—I began to refine my trust-building with teens. While clinical encounters allowed me to attend to young people's physical needs, medical treatment was only one aspect of the care they required. By taking an active role in guiding them through their anxieties or fears, I realized many of my adolescent patients saw me in the same light as I once viewed my own mentors; by listening to their aspirations and offering them just a little extra attention, I could help inspire them to pursue and realize their own dreams. This lesson stayed with me, and I began considering ways that I might incorporate adolescent care into some part of my future, even though I knew full-time pediatrics wasn't for me.

In fairness to my inpatient pediatrics rotation, I didn't get the full four-week experience due to a unique educational opportunity. At the time, I was serving as student council president of Howard's College of Medicine, and one of our officers suggested we travel to Cuba alongside a group of students from the School of Law. Back then, travel from the US to Cuba was still highly restricted and required dispensation from the US Department of Treasury's Office of Foreign Assets Control. The law students had received the necessary clearance, and thanks to further assistance from Foreign Assets Control, a chartered commercial airplane had been arranged to fly the group directly to Havana's José Martí Airport. While the law students had done the necessary groundwork, in my eyes, a trip to Cuba was still a longshot for us medical students: Could we successfully pitch the trip as being meaningful enough to warrant being excused for it? Who would go and how would we get away from our rotations? Would we have to make up the time away? Although I wasn't confident we could get approval, I was tasked with making the ask to the dean of the medical college. To my surprise, he endorsed the trip, removed roadblocks to our participation, and assigned one of his associate deans, Dr. Dawn L. Cannon, to go with the three of us to Havana. Today, I'm grateful to my classmates for motivating me to speak to the dean, and for the support we received from the faculty.

Our week in Cuba was unforgettable. From the music to the schoolchildren to the athletes in boxing rings or on baseball diamonds, the country and its culture were robust and beautiful. There were few public restaurants but no shortage of private restaurants in the kitchens of neighborhood homes, where we were treated to authentic dishes like empanadas, Cuban-style paella, and freshly caught lobster, and I couldn't help but fall in love with the people of Cuba. While we shared most cultural experiences with the (much larger) group of law students, the four of us from the medical school were given tours of various healthcare sites courtesy of Cuba's Ministry of Public Health. Because Cuba's national health system was widely developed, with free, prevention-focused healthcare available to all, many clinics were nestled into communities across the island, and local physicians and nurses greeted us warmly and took the time to speak with us. One highlight of the trip was our tour of the Latin American School of Medical Sciences (later renamed the Latin American School of Medicine); the school had opened in Havana only a year or two prior, and it was attracting students from Central America, South America, the Caribbean, and other areas. Judging from the many smiles we saw on the tour, the Cuban people took great pride in their role in improving healthcare across so many countries and regions.

Cuba's nationalized healthcare system was successful in many ways, but access to the latest medical technology was limited, and the country's overall infrastructure needed modernization. When we visited one major hospital in Havana, intermittent power outages—and no hospital-wide backup generators—potentially left patients in operating rooms or on ventilators at risk. Back at our hotel, hot water was an amenity, and it was available only during certain hours of the day. Fidel Castro and his communist regime still loomed large over the country, to the point of demagoguery. Both then and now, because physicians are paid by the state at a set rate, and because no private clinics are allowed in the country, doctors generally aren't financially well off despite their vast knowledge. (To the point where, before I went home, I left a pair of Nike sneakers with a doctor who couldn't afford them, which was humbling.) At the same time, though, my classmates and I were at a formative stage in our education, and visiting Cuba offered us insight into the practice of medicine in a culture and country different from our own.

Cuba felt like a rotation onto itself, but above all it solidified for me the importance of a robust public health system and access to healthcare services for all. Because the foundational years of my medical training were in Washington, DC—the seat of our nation's government—I saw

firsthand the juxtaposition between doctors who improved health patient by patient and the large-scale government decisions/actions that
could change the trajectory of health and healthcare for millions. I
challenged myself to carefully contemplate the ways I might better prepare myself to answer a calling that perhaps was even bigger than my
initial dreams.

I rotated through several other clerkships during my third year,
and each helped me discover which aspects of clinical care I was more
naturally suited to. The faster-paced, heavily-patient-facing rotations
captivated me the most, as I had an insatiable desire to be where the
action was. No matter which specialty I was rotating through, I found
crossover opportunities to work with trauma and EM teams to learn
as much as possible about urgent and acute care. As my third year of
school came to a close in 2001, after many, many discussions with
mentors, advisors, and peers, I finally came to understand that one
specialty had been calling to me all along: emergency medicine.

CHAPTER 9

The Clinical Years of Medical School: Keeping My Eyes on the Prize

IN THE MID-SUMMER OF 2001, AFTER ONLY TWO OR THREE WEEKS OFF to recharge, I returned to HUH to complete my clinical years. With a strong foundation in gross anatomy and pathology from my science courses, I was prepared for my fourth-year advanced surgery rotation. Surgery was the most-revered rotation at HUH, and we were taught by stalwarts in medicine such as Dr. Clive Callender, the third African American transplant surgeon in the nation and founder of Howard's transplant program, and neurosurgeon Dr. Gary Dennis, a former president of the National Medical Association. This rotation taught my peers and me core principles of surgery like *primum non nocere* (first do no harm). While we performed the typical scut work assigned to students and spent time observing in the operating room, the gem of the experience for me was far less about learning surgical techniques and far more about the perseverance, excellence, humility, and accountability HUH surgeons constantly displayed. For example, it wasn't uncommon for an attending surgeon to stay overnight in the hospital out of concern for a critical patient who might need to be brought back into the OR at a moment's notice. On occasions when multiple trauma activations required emergency surgery, a senior resident would start a surgical case while the attending was in an adjacent OR with the most critical patient. Their dedication humbled me, and watching the surgical team practice their craft broadened the aperture through which I viewed patient care.

My advanced surgical rotation at Howard had two primary components: emergency trauma care and general surgery. Like my classmates, I was on call every fourth or fifth day, and this is when I was on the trauma side of the rotation and stationed in the ER. Of all the experiences I had while on trauma, the most memorable one occurred when a transgender woman was brought into the trauma bay after being found beaten and stabbed in the bushes. She was unconscious and barely breathing, and she was quickly intubated. In my surgical team's initial examination of this patient, we found more than ten stab wounds in her abdomen along with internal bleeding. Covered in dirt and grass and left to die, this woman had been attacked for nothing more than being her authentic self. This senseless attack—a reality too common for marginalized people—turned my stomach, even as I was humbled, once again, by the fragility of human life. I pushed the thought aside for the moment, knowing I could pray on it later—right now every second counted. Doing my part to save her, I successfully placed an IV line in her left arm. I then worked with a nurse to get the line connected, and I squeezed a liter bag of saline with my hand to push fluids into her system. That was my contribution as a medical student; the residents placed chest tubes to reinflate her collapsed lungs before rushing her to the operating room.

In the trauma bay, I felt as close to the front lines as possible without being outside of the hospital. Here, people from all cultures, races, and socioeconomic backgrounds found themselves blindsided by a health crisis, and I found immense satisfaction in helping them through their most critical moments. For my classmates and me, our job was two-fold. We needed to a) learn how to bring calm and certainty to chaotic and often life-threatening situations, and b) acquire an understanding of rapid patient assessment (and delivery of quality treatment) while keeping a cool head and extending empathy to those we were treating. I felt this is where I could shine. Building on the skills I'd learned during my internal medicine rotation, I even convinced some of the ER nurses to let me get in on the action and place large-bore IVs when needed, a procedure I became skilled at. I also managed the treatment of those in the surgical intensive care units, where many post-op patients needed to stay for extended periods of time. Overall, the rotation affirmed for me that my decision to pursue an EM residency was well chosen: even though I liked going into the OR to observe, when intraoperative op-portunities arose, I was happy to defer to my classmates who wanted to specialize in general surgery. The more time I spent on the trauma bay, the more crisis patients I could help, and the more I could learn, even if only by proxy, about emergency medicine.

It was late August when I began my EM clerkship. I'd elected to take this rotation early in the year; to apply to EM residencies in the fall, I needed a recommendation letter and a strong evaluation from an EM attending. The clerkship was what I expected it to be: outstanding clinical exposure alongside unparalleled instruction. On this rotation, I was able, for the first time, to place a central venous catheter in a patient's femoral vein without assistance. (Placing this catheter is common in emergency situations and is an important competency for any doctor in EM.) I'd learned this procedure during my surgical rotation. After I'd walked through every single step needed and reviewed all potential complications with my attending, she—instead of donning a gown and gloves and then positioning herself near me in the sterile field—stood in the corner and allowed me to perform the placement by myself. For me, this was a huge accomplishment and confidence booster. While I still had much to learn, I was making recognizable progress, and this did not go unnoticed by some of the residents to whom I looked up.

Unlike in most other specialties, EM physicians work in clinical shifts, ensuring around-the-clock physician coverage of the emergency department. As such, residents and medical students worked various shifts as well. While the day and evening shifts were not too disruptive to my sleep patterns, I did have to learn how to nap or sleep during the day so I could be awake all night. Working the night shift was very different from being on call during overnight hours; those on call could get some sleep with the hope of not being awoken too many times, but those on the night shift needed to be fully awake. The night shift came with yet another challenge too, as nearly every doctor a student might turn to for a consult was on the other side of the circadian fence—and every single one of them was hoping *not* to be called upon.

I was on this rotation when I faced one of the most daunting days of my life. On September 10th, 2001, I came into the emergency department for my overnight shift as scheduled. The next morning, toward the end of the night shift, my team rounded with the incoming day team as usual to ensure proper continuity of patient care. With rounds complete, my team and I hung around and chatted a bit, while Dr.

Labat (who was an EM attending by this time and was scheduled to continue working through the day shift) went to her first meeting of the day, which was in a conference room with a TV. Moments later, just before 9:00 a.m., she hurried out of the room looking stunned: in New York City, a hijacked airplane had crashed into one of the World Trade Center's Twin Towers.

Not fully grasping what was happening, I went home and tuned into the news. In utter dismay I watched the horror of the September 11th attacks unfold. In the time it had taken me to get home, a second plane had hit the remaining Twin Tower, and mere moments after I'd walked in the door, a third had hit the Pentagon. In the city where I felt protected, in the seat of our nation's government, everything had suddenly changed in one morning. Our nation was under attack, and later that morning I learned a fourth plane (which I now know the hijackers intended to crash into a DC target—a plan that was heroically thwarted by the passengers aboard[12]) had crashed in rural Pennsylvania. Like most Americans, I hadn't known what it felt like to be under foreign attack in our homeland. I'd driven by the Pentagon many times on the way to an area mall, the Fashion Centre at Pentagon City, never imagining that the Pentagon would be the site of such a horrendous attack. A part of me was numb; the rest of me was processing the reality and trying to predict the unknown.

I tried many times to call friends and family, but both landline- and cellphone-service were out, either as a direct result of the attacks or for security reasons. I got little rest that day, but at some point in the af-

---

12 The Washington Post: <https://wapo.st/3KzmW3i>

ternoon, I managed to fall asleep so I could be ready for my next night shift. From all I'd seen on the news, the casualty count from the attacks was undeniably catastrophic, and I assumed overflow patients from the Pentagon were being distributed to various DC hospitals. Yet it was eerily quiet in the emergency department that night; very few patients came in. One of the attendings on shift that night was the medical director of DC's Fire and Emergency Medical Services Department, and he was in the know: HUH had received no overflow patients because the attack on the Pentagon had so few survivors.

This was an especially frightening time for the nation's capital. Many DC residents felt that our city was one of the safest places in the world, yet the nerve center of our military forces had been attacked, and so many innocent lives had been ripped away from us. Only a week later, another frightening saga started to unfold: letters laced with anthrax began circulating in the US mail system, with at least two of them being sent to Capitol Hill and contaminating much of DC.[13] For weeks, I opened my mail over a trashcan outside my apartment while wearing an N95 respirator mask. During that time, I began to grasp the very real possibility that, at some point in my future as an EM physician, I might have to care for patients from a mass-casualty event, or I might even find myself on the frontlines treating victims after a bioterrorism attack. The responsibility awed me.

A few months later, when it was time for me to begin interviewing for residency placement (a process that often requires travel), the typical traffic delays around Reagan National Airport had vanished,

---

13   The University of California, Los Angles: <https://bit.ly/39vlMrQ>

and the airport itself was largely empty. Security protocols were at an all-time high, and few planes were allowed in or out of Reagan National. For those planes that did get permission to fly, air marshals were assigned to almost every flight, and in-air security was strict: in the last thirty minutes of any flight, passengers were not allowed out of their seats for any reason. Per Secretary of Defense Donald Rumsfeld's order, any plane—if hijacked—could be fired upon by the Air Force if the president couldn't be immediately reached.[14] On my returning flights to DC, as we entered the flight-restricted zone, in the back of my mind I wondered if an unruly passenger mistaken for a hijacker could cause my flight to be shot down.

Fear of other airplanes being hijacked and used as weapons, on top of growing global terrorism concerns, led to my international away rotation in Germany with the Asclepios Telemedicine/Telecare Exchange Program being canceled. Instead, I clerked out of Howard's Telehealth Science and the Advanced Technology Center, which was across the street from the medical school in Howard's brand-new Louis Stokes Health Sciences Library. Under the direction of Dr. Ernest Carter, MD, PhD, we partnered with an academic medical institution in Africa with the goal of better facilitating international consultations. As a student, I was afforded a view into the future of healthcare delivery. To manage clinical care, we used first-gen digital medical devices alongside a nascent patient-profile portal. Although the technology we piloted wasn't without the blips common to the era, the Internet was increasingly connecting people across the globe. Dr. Carter's vision was to

---

14   The Washington Post: <https://wapo.st/3745dDu>

set up a new digital infrastructure that could connect medical experts at Howard with both colleagues and patients around the world. Even amid all the tension and fear in DC at that time, he continued working to make healthcare more accessible to all. Today, Dr. Carter continues his work as the Health Officer of Prince George's County Health Department in Maryland.

The September 11th attacks threw a major curveball into my fourth year, but it was certainly a period in my life I will never forget. Despite the upheaval, I did complete all my clerkships on time, including a radiology elective that combined my love of anatomy with imaging technology. (In fact, for a short while, I considered specializing in radiology, but one of my pediatrics attendings, Dr. Sandra Ford, shot the idea down, saying that my bedside skills were too strong to enter a specialty with such limited patient interaction.) Like I had the year before, when rotations took me away from urgent and acute care, I found opportunities to get myself back into the ER. In a way, I'd started my career training even before being placed into a residency, and I felt my skills in this area were strong. My path to physicianship was, at long last, finally clear to me.

When I started my journey to becoming a physician, I didn't have a clear understanding of every leg of the race. I knew about college, medical school, and residency, but the number of years required for each made the steps seem too far apart to be real. But then, somehow much sooner than expected, I was in my fourth year of medical school, and it was time to start applying to residency training programs.

One unique component of the fourth year is that, on top of required clerkships, it includes a job hunt from October through January. (A residency is both a training program and a paid position.) I had some familiarity with the components of the residency search: a nationwide system, the Electronic Residency Application Service (ERAS) that connects graduating students with open positions; every residency is linked to a specific specialty and lasts one to seven years depending on that specialty; interviews can lead candidates to hospitals anywhere in the country. Successful placement in a program is known as Matching, and Matches are announced in March, with residencies usually beginning during the tail-end of June.

Matching successfully would perhaps be the most consequential leg of my journey, although each step is important in its own right. Every medical student graduates knowing about the same amount of information yet has limited skill in clinical practice and caring for patients—it's the residency training process that has the most significant differentiating effect on a physician's career. Having decided that EM would be my specialty of choice, I was aiming for the best of all worlds for my training: a top hospital, an excellent EM program, a vibrant and diverse city, and the ability to serve communities in need. However, because placements at the best hospitals are highly competitive, I had no guarantee that I would Match into any of my top-three programs. With a job hunt looming over my final year of school, I found myself at yet another transition point that held both promise and uncertainty.

In the fall, I began putting together my ERAS package. Clerkship grades, scores on licensing exams, and research experience were of course heavily weighted by residency programs, as were letters of recommendation and the personal essay. To discover where some of the best EM programs were located, and to learn how to present myself as a competitive candidate, I reached out to my network, including faculty at Howard's College of Medicine. Around this time, my senior advisor, Dr. Dawn L. Cannon, counseled me to include Chicago on the list of cities for my search, prompting me to begin applying to programs there immediately. Largely because of my ongoing interest in public health policy and healthcare reform, I also knew business school was likely in my future after residency, so I considered programs that could help me make this transition. In my ERAS personal essay, I wrote:

> As an emergency medicine physician, I look forward to serving a patient population that extends beyond most social and economic boundaries. [...] I will thrive off of the challenges of my profession, from the puzzling presentation of a patient to the need for physician and patient advocacy on Capitol Hill.
>
> While patient care will remain at the center of my career, I also plan to pursue my interests in healthcare delivery systems and public policy. To this end, I plan to pursue a master's degree in business administration after completing my residency training. As the medical arena continues to evolve, I want to be prepared to encounter it at any level and on any stage.

My residency interviews spanned from November 2001 to January 2002, and my travels came with new cities and new faces all across the nation. I interviewed at programs in Los Angeles, Houston, Jacksonville, Columbus, Detroit, St. Louis, Chicago, and Baltimore. I was hoping that perhaps my placement in a program would take me back to the warmer weather of the south, but I was not invited to interview at well-regarded programs in Atlanta and New Orleans. Clearly, fate was telling me that it was time to spread my wings and fly in a brand-new direction.

One especially memorable trip was to Los Angeles, where I interviewed at the EM program at the Martin Luther King Jr./Drew Medical Center (King/Drew), located in my Uncle James' neighborhood. When I arrived at the airport, my older cousin Kenny picked me up. He had a big, infectious smile that stretched from ear to ear, and even at this first in-person meeting as adults, I could tell he was a really cool guy. Unfortunately, however, like many young Black men in South Central Los Angeles, Kenny had been sucked into street life as a teenager; both he and his older brother (nicknamed Scooter) ended up spending many of their prime years in prison. While I'd always known of Kenny through the family grapevine, I had no memory of the times we'd met when I was very young, and now it was great to see him at home with his parents and family. Yet at the same time, meeting him was bittersweet since I would never be able to meet Scooter, who had reformed after prison only to be tragically murdered. After being shot, Scooter had been rushed to King/Drew, but the physicians couldn't save his life. This gave me a unique, personal connection to King/Drew, and my family was proud of me for interviewing at an institution so steeped in fighting the epidemic of gun violence.

By the end of the interview season, I felt that any number of programs could be right for me, and I entered my ranking preferences into the Match's electronic system. Yet one program enticed me above all others: the EM residency at the University of Chicago (UChicago). If accepted into the program, I would rotate through multiple hospital sites, from academic medical centers to safety-net hospitals. As a world-class institution, the University of Chicago Hospital was (and is still) at the forefront of innovation and technology, and the EM program director unabashedly embraced racial diversity in trainees. (The program director is the physician in charge of a residency program's overall educational mission.) The program came strongly recommended to me by Dr. Richard Watson, a Howard alum and former chief resident in the program, and it offered excellent cross-specialty training for off-service rotations like cardiology and critical care. Additionally, through a series of calls and emails, I had formed a strong relationship with the program's director during the interview season. However, because of the strict procedures surrounding the Match process, I couldn't be one-hundred percent sure that I would land this residency position. All I could do, like every other member of my class, was cross my fingers and wait.

On Match Day 2002, with only weeks to go until graduation, I put on my poker face to hide my nerves as our dean welcomed us to the morning's ceremony. His congratulatory speech was only a few minutes long, yet I had to work to keep cool, knowing all the while that the next three years of my life were inside the envelope in my hand. The second we were given permission, I tore open my Match envelope and scanned the letter inside. I was Chicago-bound!

CHAPTER 10

When the ER Became My Classroom

WITH MY MEDICAL DEGREE IN HAND, MY MOTHER AND UNCLE HELPED me pack up my belongings in DC and hit the road. While my pre-moving aspiration had been to buy a home in Chicago, I wasn't able to find an affordable, well-maintained property at that time. However, UChicago graduate housing was available for first-year residents, and I took advantage of this fallback option. It was a warm summer evening when I arrived at my new home—a small, one-bedroom apartment in a vintage building—in Chicago's Hyde Park community. It was strange moving in; the bathroom fixtures were old-fashioned, and the claw-foot bathtub was really deep. When I filled the tub with tap water (which came from Lake Michigan), the water actually looked blue.

Chicago was beautiful, and people were everywhere. My neighborhood was walkable, and a stunning lakefront view was just a few blocks away from my apartment. In fact, when John, one of my fellow first-year residents, suggested I buy a bike so we could ride along the lakefront path and take in the summertime scenes, it didn't take much convincing before I started bike shopping. Summer was absolutely the best time to be in Chicago with one exception: my apartment didn't have air conditioning.

My first week on the job involved a slew of orientation activities, but afterward I quickly transitioned into clinical rotations at UChicago Hospital and its affiliates. I'd enjoyed getting to know all the first-year residents in the program, but after orientation week we were dispersed across various services at various hospitals. Practically speaking, I knew we would only see each other at our weekly departmental meetings, which typically lasted about three hours and were led by our program director. In addition to these meetings, department faculty members gave weekly lectures to reinforce the curriculum. This helped ensure that all residents achieved the specific academic and clinical competencies that were required during each step of residency.

My first rotation was in Mitchell Hospital's emergency department. (Today, UChicago's Adult ED is connected to the Center for Care and Discovery by an enclosed footbridge.) Mitchell was the preeminent teaching location for our program, and it was where patients with complex medical conditions were sent for treatment. (Some of these conditions were so rare or complex that normally residents wouldn't encounter them until after completing their training.) As an intern (i.e., a first-year resident), I became proficient in a wide range of EM procedures. Any time a patient came in crashing or in need of a specific procedure, the senior residents would seek out interns to ensure our first-year training was as hands-on as possible. It wasn't uncommon for interns like me to be fully engrossed in repairing a complex laceration, yet at the same time, we needed to be efficient in our care so we wouldn't miss out on key learning opportunities as new patients came into the ER.

Our waiting room was full almost twenty-three hours a day, with our slow period being from 5:30 a.m. to 6:45 a.m. each day. Most patients waited a long time for care, and they had many, many questions. Initially, when I walked into a room to interview and examine a patient, it was very difficult for me to close out the exam without first hearing a bevy of concerns—whether they were related to the reason for the visit or not—that the patient (and family members) had. Until I learned how to properly steer a patient interview, this made me pretty inefficient as an EM practitioner. With a little practice, however, I did learn to keep the interview focused while gathering a solid history of the complaint. Normally, if a patient came in with a headache (a type of bread-and-butter presentation in the ER), I would assess the issue from all angles: intensity of the pain; the pace of onset; the pain's character (sharp, dull, shooting, throbbing, etc.); actions that made the headache better or worse; the presence of associated symptoms like nausea, vomiting, numbness, dizziness, or weakness. This intense, thorough approach often exposed the root of the pain, but, if not, I would send the patient for tests to detect or exclude the possibility of life-threatening causes.

Airway management was among the first key skills I needed to master. Back then, emergency management technicians (EMTs) commonly used a type of airway called a Combitube, which could be inserted blindly (without visualizing the airway) by a tech to mechanically ventilate a patient. However, the Combitube is for temporary use only; a physician trained in endotracheal tube placement (i.e., intubation performed under direct visualization of the airway) must replace it as soon as possible. Interns, under the watchful eyes of senior residents or attendings, were routinely called to the head of the bed to manage a patient's airway. My first ER intubation involved a cardiac-arrest patient who'd had a Combitube placed. I felt up to the challenge, but I was too green to know that vomiting was common upon the removal of the temporary tube. I worked carefully, but the next thing I knew, an eruption of vomit spewed from my patient. I narrowly escaped an unpleasant shower, and as I looked at the nurses, I suddenly realized that I was lucky to walk away with my white coat still clean.

Every day in the ER was different, but without exception, I saw patients with complex mental health issues, STDs, lacerations requiring repair, and other cases that more-senior residents had graduated from treating. On those occasions when a patient passed away, it was also usually an intern's job to break the news to the family. (Even to this day, telling a family their loved one has died remains the hardest part of the job—it never really gets any easier.) While it may seem odd for interns to be tasked with this solemn duty, developing an extremely high level of empathy is among the first lessons residents need to learn. Grasping the true gravity of a physician's role needs to be learned early, and it should guide any doctor throughout the whole of their career.

Of these heart-wrenching conversations, one of the hardest I ever had as an intern came after I'd had the privilege of caring for a mother in her mid-thirties. A few days earlier, my patient had had arthroscopic knee surgery, and she'd come to the ER because of pain and swelling in the calf of her post-operative leg. After examining her, I was confident that she'd developed a blood clot in her leg. While she didn't present chest pain or difficulty breathing (signs that a clot had traveled to her lungs), her heart rate was elevated. I ordered a CT scan of her chest, and to address the clot itself, I prescribed and immediately administered the standard course of treatment: a blood thinner. During the hour or so we waited for radiology to call upstairs, I learned my patient's mom, a nurse, would be coming to the ED to be with her daughter.

The transport service arrived. Wheeling a patient from ED to radiology typically took about five minutes, so I was surprised when, only ten minutes later, a radiology technician called to tell me my patient was confused and disoriented. Alarm shot through me—she'd been completely coherent when she'd left the ED. I ran down to radiology to find my patient sitting up on her gurney, short of breath and confused. We rushed her back upstairs, moving as swiftly as safety allowed.

The instant we arrived in the ED, my patient went into cardiac arrest—it was that fast. A senior resident and I began CPR. I intubated her, then called down to the pharmacy for a special clot-busting medication to push through her IV. Frantic, we worked on her for forty-five minutes, but we couldn't get our patient back. Just after pronouncing her dead, we pulled back the privacy curtain only to find her mother walking toward us. Before I'd even taken in the reality of losing my patient, the mother's anguish gutted me. She'd come to the ED with the expectation of comforting her daughter, never expecting to find her child gone, her grandchildren instantly made motherless. Nothing I could say or do would make it better, all I could offer this mother was compassion.

One of the daily obligations I met in the ER was providing care for patients who had nowhere else to go. This was especially true during my residency years, as they preceded the Affordable Care Act (ACA) reforms of 2010.[15] (Despite the ACA, a lack of health insurance still

---

15 The Affordable Care Act of 2010, commonly known as Obamacare, expanded access to health insurance for millions of Americans. At the time of this writing, over thirty million Americans are enrolled in ACA programs. See Whitehouse.gov: <https://bit.ly/38DYhOk>

persists today. Additionally, some people who are insured can't afford the high deductibles required of their health plans; therefore, they defer treatment until a crisis arises.[16]) Treating those with limited healthcare options was a driving force behind my becoming a doctor, and the uninsured in particular need the safety net that ERs provide.

For vulnerable populations who rarely, if ever, see doctors, the ER can mean the difference between life and death—even when a patient's initial presentation seems relatively benign. I learned this first-hand when an unkempt man arrived in the ER late one evening with tooth pain, a fever, neck pain, and foul breath. He smelled like smoke, and he had burns on his fingertips. I knew such burns were a telltale sign of crack cocaine use, as users often singe themselves on the glass pipes they use to smoke the drug. My patient admitted to having a crack addiction, and he noted that his drug use temporarily eased the extreme dental pain he'd been suffering with for months.

There's nothing like a toothache to get someone's attention. Even though many of us don't think of oral hygiene and routine dental cleanings as being integral to overall health, plenty of medical conditions can arise from neglected oral hygiene, as the mouth is a gateway to the body. This was certainly true for my patient, who, like many marginalized people, hadn't been to the dentist for years. (To complicate matters, his ongoing dental issues were exacerbated by his crack use.) As I began my exam, I saw that his tongue was elevated; he had an unusual redness spreading across his mouth, and there were pockets of puss caused by his dental infection. When I asked him to say

---

16 The Houston Chronicle: <https://bit.ly/3OPqL81>

"ah," he was unable to fully open his mouth, and I couldn't see the structures at the back of the throat. Additionally, the skin between his neck and collarbone was hot and discolored, and when I touched it, I felt a crackling, popping sensation. My heart rate quickened. This was subcutaneous crepitus (abnormal air/gas under the skin) brought on by a bacterial gangrene; that gangrene was causing his flesh to die and release gas or air. This, plus the inflammation across his mouth and under his tongue, meant my patient's airway could swell shut within a matter of hours.

This was a surgical emergency, but since my patient wasn't short of breath yet, I ordered a quick CT scan. The results confirmed my diagnosis: the infection had spread from his mouth, down through the muscles in his neck, and into the mediastinum at the middle of the chest. I had to move quickly. After consulting with my attending and senior resident, we decided to take advantage of the little time we had by placing a breathing tube before the patient entered respiratory distress. We called for the ED's difficult-airway cart immediately. While we would usually fully sedate and medically paralyze a patient before an emergency intubation, this patient needed to be awake and breathing on his own due to the significant swelling. To manage the discomfort this procedure would cause, we chose a combination of topical and aerosolized anesthetics on the structures of his throat. This approach was necessary because sedation could cause his airway to collapse before we were able to successfully place the endotracheal tube; if this happened, the patient would go into cardiac arrest.

Among the critical tools on the cart was a fiberoptic scope, which is a thin black tube with a light and camera on the end that's connected to a monitor. While I'd used fiberoptic scopes fairly routinely, this case was high-risk and would test all that I'd learned. I called on all my experience to advance the scope through my patient's left nostril, navigate it past the curve in the back of the nose, move it downward to the pharynx, and maneuver it behind the epiglottis, which is just above the vocal cords. I then moved the scope down between his vocal cords into the trachea before I slid an endotracheal tube over the top of the scope and advanced it to the exact same location. I removed the scope while leaving the breathing tube behind, protecting my patient from the impending closing of his natural airway. As I'd worked, various surgeons had arrived in the ER; in essence, I'd thankfully had an audience of more experienced physicians around me. With the airway secured, we were then able to sedate the patient. After a quick assessment, the surgical team brought him to the operating room, where they removed a significant amount of dead tissue from his neck and chest and performed a tracheostomy. If the ER had not been open and accessible to all, this patient surely would've died that day.

Working in a large ER means serving patients in any way possible, and that includes transporting in critical patients from *other* hospitals if necessary. When a patient at a community hospital is critically ill and their needs exceed the capabilities of their facility, it's not uncommon for the patient to be transferred to an academic medical center for more-advanced or more-specialized treatment. At UChicago, our transport service was staffed with both a nurse and a resident, and the service employed both ambulances and a hospital-owned helicopter. Second- and third-year residents working in the ER were also on call for the transport service, which meant, among other things, that we needed to constantly communicate our patients' cases and needs to the staff on shift, meticulously update all and any documentation after every bedside check, and ensure our patients were nicely tucked in, as there was always a chance that we would need to transition them to another doctor at a moment's notice. In addition to patient transfers, anyone on the transport service had to be ready to act for on-scene responses (i.e., severe accidents or other disasters) at all times. It was impossible to estimate how many calls the transport service might receive in a single shift—sometimes a shift wouldn't have a single transfer, while others had multiple transfers. It was also impossible to predict the types of cases we would encounter while on a transport—from babies to adults, from those with complex treatment needs to acute trauma victims, we brought many to UChicago in the hope of getting them the care they needed.

During one overnight shift, my transport pager went off at 3:00 a.m. It hadn't been a bad night in the ER; things were under control, and despite the storm raging outside, all was relatively calm on the floor. At the beeping of my pager, I signed my patients over to a colleague, and within ten minutes, I was in an advanced-life-support ambulance, headed to a hospital about forty minutes away. A ride in the back of an ambulance with a critical care nurse during a rainstorm wasn't exactly how I'd envisioned spending my night, but a patient needed heart surgery urgently, and it was my job to help him. As was usual for transport calls, I'd been given limited information about the patient, but I noticed we had an intra-aortic balloon pump (which assists in feeding the vessels of the heart with blood) and other highly specialized equipment in the ambulance, which was a sign of the severity of the patient's illness.

We arrived at the community hospital and passed through the fairly busy ER, and I waved hello to a friend who was the attending physician that night. Crammed into an elevator with our gurney, machines, and resuscitation-medication bags, we headed upstairs to the ICU where three nurses were preparing the patient for the transfer. They handed the transport nurse syringes with various heart-stabilizing medications and programed the patient's IV lines to administer continuous drips. Boxes of opened atropine and epinephrine were on hand as the patient's heart had stopped less than an hour before our arrival, requiring brief CPR.

Due to his severe heart failure, the patient was on a balloon pump like the one we had in the ambulance. A final step in our transfer process was to switch him over to our pump, which I did carefully but quickly. With that done, I made a call to Mitchell with an update, and we checked the patient's vitals to ensure he was stable. As we left the ICU, an aery look of relief painted the nurses' faces—they'd been working hard to care for this patient, and they were drained. We wheeled the patient to the elevator bank when suddenly his monitors began beeping wildly. We had a problem. The patient's heart rate had shot up, and within seconds, his heart entered a potentially fatal arrhythmia.

Calling out for a crash cart, we retraced our twenty-second path back to the ICU. "It's happening again!" yelled a nurse. We began chest compressions, defibrillated (shocked) the patient, administered the necessary drugs, and checked the settings on all our equipment. After another round of medications and several minutes of CPR, we had a pulse again. I breathed a sigh of relief, yet I began to wonder if transporting this patient now was the right thing to do: Had we set realistic expectations for his family? Should he have been transferred earlier? By this time it was 4:30 a.m., and I called his family to explain the stark reality of the situation, and I also called his attending physician to ensure we were on the same page. We made a collective decision to continue with the transfer. Given the limited care options at the community hospital, leaving the patient, however tenuously stable, would most likely result in death.

With sweat on our brows from performing CPR, we again left the ICU, then got on the elevator. When the doors opened on the ground floor, we felt like we'd made some progress. Navigating the quiet, fluorescent-lit hallways, we proceeded methodically through the hospital's corridors and back to the ER. Our ambulance driver was walking about fifteen yards in front of us—he planned to open the ambulance's doors ahead of our arrival. With the exit to the ER in sight, I thought we were in the clear. I was wrong. Without warning, our patient coded again.

This was quickly becoming a nightmare. We rushed to the ER's resuscitation room and ran the code again, but this time we needed fifteen minutes and multiple defibrillations to get the patient's heartbeat back. As I caught my breath, my friend (the ER's attending) shook her head and gave me a supportive thumbs up. She knew what we were up against—and we still had a forty-minute drive ahead of us. Just then, as I began to refocus on getting the patient to our ambulance, I heard the low-grade rumble of a helicopter. During our clinical storm, the stormy skies outside had cleared, and the rain was gone. The ambulance driver had called back to dispatch during our last resuscitation, and UChicago's helicopter was cleared to pick us up. The helipad of this hospital was on the ground level, about twenty-five yards from the ER's ambulance entrance. Other than my very first ride-along, I'd never been more thrilled to load up into a helicopter. We took off as quickly as possible and accelerated into the dawn of a new morning, with the sun rising over Lake Michigan and the Chicago skyline in the distance.

Hugging the shoreline, we flew for seven or eight minutes. On our final approach to Mitchell's helipad, we began slowing down, and everyone fell quiet per landing protocols. Suddenly, the patient coded for a third time. His heart was in ventricular tachycardia, and his blood pressure was tanking. With the helicopter yet to touch down on the rooftop, I delivered a swift precordial thump to his chest, then followed it with a defibrillation administered through the electrode pads we'd adhered to his chest during our prior CPR. As soon as we'd landed safely, I radioed for a resuscitation team, then I began chest compressions. By the time the decelerating rotor blades above us stopped spinning, the team met us. They revived the patient and rushed him to the heart cath lab. My heart went out to the patient and his family.

I had many memorable patient-care experiences during my three years as a resident. The emergency department is a unique learning environment, and it truly became my classroom all throughout my specialty training. As a young physician, I landed in a proving ground, one where I had to simultaneously respect and appreciate the experience of the nurses I worked with (some of whom had cared for patients longer than I'd been alive), yet simultaneously develop the clinical acumen and confidence to make decisions in the best interest of my patients. Humility was an early and recurring lesson; as much as EM residents like me aimed to diagnose ailments with both swiftness and precision, we often didn't have comprehensive patient profiles to guide us—and time to contemplate our decisions was a luxury we rarely had. Whether it was sizing up a mentally unstable patient who needed some space and medications for everyone's safety or listening to a gut feeling, there was a lot to learn that wasn't written in any textbook. Every day brought a new challenge, and the range of emotions I experienced as a resident, coupled with the many high-stress situations endemic to any ER, was sobering. Becoming an expert in EM required a maturity I never could've anticipated as a medical student, and I found myself growing as both a doctor and a human being every day.

CHAPTER 11

A Transformative Twenty-Four Hours

UCHICAGO's EM PROGRAM OFFERED A BEVY OF OPPORTUNITIES FOR residents, including the chance to attend a few medical conferences per year, and I took full advantage of this whenever I could. During my final residency summer in July 2004, I was scheduled, along with a few peers from my program, to attend a conference in San Diego. Because direct flights to Los Angeles were less expensive than flights to San Diego, my good friend, fellow resident, and fraternity brother Dr. John Fisher and I decided to fly into LAX, pay my uncle James in South Central a quick visit, hang out in Los Angeles for the day, then drive down to the conference.

I was looking forward to a few days' leave from the ER when my mom called with devastating news: my cousin Kenny had been shot and killed. My heart broke. Kenny and his friend had been sitting in his car, in the driveway of his parents' home, when a stranger ran up and murdered them both in a brutal, targeted attack. At the time, Kenny's parents (i.e., my uncle James and his wife) and one of his sons, Little Kenny, were inside the house; the shooting was as little as fifteen feet from the front door.

The pain and loss my family faced remains indescribable. While no one (to my knowledge) was ever charged for Kenny's murder, the fact remains that Kenny had gone down a rough path as a teenager, and his murder was likely linked to his past gang affiliation. I've never known the exact circumstances of his history, but even back then, I knew Kenny had worked hard to reform himself after prison. Losing him to the street life he'd denounced was so unfair; my uncle and aunt had lost both of their children to gun violence; and Kenny's daughter and two sons had become fatherless with just the pull of a trigger.

Kenny and I had only just begun getting to know each other as adults in the last few years, but our bond was fast, and I needed to attend his services. By some twist of fate, his funeral was being held on the same day John and I were planning to be in Los Angeles. We canceled our relaxing day of sightseeing, and John kindly agreed to attend Kenny's memorial with me. I needed to pay my respects, but I also knew I wouldn't have much time with my family since John and I had to drive to our San Diego conference directly from Kenny's homegoing.

The sunny skies that greeted us as we approached Los Angeles contrasted with the soberness now underlying the trip. At LAX, John and I grabbed a rental car and drove straight to the funeral home. As we pulled up, the parking lot was full. Many people were outside, some wearing T-shirts adorned with Kenny's picture. People from all walks of life had come out to pay their respects and offer condolences to the family. While the outpouring offered some solace, during the services I found my eyes drawn to Little Kenny, who was seated a few rows ahead and was but a young teenager at the time. My heart ached for him even as my brain struggled with a stark reality: the systemic violence of

South Central could suck him in too, and the possibility wasn't even all that unlikely. Undoubtedly, neighborhood rumors speculating about who pulled the trigger would begin circulating soon enough; it was impossible for me to predict if or how the cycle of anger, peer pressure, and expectation of retaliation would play out for Little Kenny. It was a tough reality to absorb. While my faith in God remained strong, it was hard to see the Divine wisdom of taking a father away from his children, especially when they were already trying to catch up on lost time, and even more so because Little Kenny was at such a critical age. For my uncle and aunt, who'd already endured unimaginable pain as parents, no words or prayers could ever fill the shared void of their hearts.

After the funeral, John and I went to my uncle's home for the repast. The street outside his house was jammed with cars and friends, typical of a Los Angeles homegoing. Not typical was the police presence made necessary by the circumstances of Kenny's death, and no one was able to ignore the LAPD helicopter hovering above the neighborhood. This was a really sad day for me; my family's turmoil and loss enveloped me, and I felt mired by the aftermath of the same gun violence and gang warfare that plagued my patients and their communities back in Chicago. It was comforting to simply be with my family as we reflected on our good times with Kenny, his love of cooking, and his way of making us laugh or smile when we were feeling down. The suddenness of his death didn't seem real, but at the same time, I knew how things on the streets could change at a moment's notice.

John and I stayed a good while at the repast. We still had to make it to the San Diego conference, though, and when the moment seemed right, we decided that it was time to roll out. However, just before leaving, I took a photo with my family to remember the day. The loss of Kenny, plus the day itself, created a heavy load for me to bear, but fortunately our two-hour drive to San Diego allowed me some time to shift my mindset into professional mode. Dr. Hines, a mentor to both me and John, was expecting us at his pre-conference reception. For residents and medical students, his reception was not to be missed: it was always well-attended, Dr. Hines never cut corners on the catering, and coming together with peers from across the country in a social stetting was a rare opportunity. John and I had an incentive not to be too late, and we arrived around 6:30 p.m.

I couldn't have known it then, but as I walked into the reception, one of the saddest days of my life transformed into serendipity itself. Even to this day I'm still astonished: July 31st, 2004, delivered unto me both a tragic ending and a new beginning—two indelible moments on my life's journey, neither orchestrated by my own hand.

John and I grabbed some appetizers and found our group of friends from Chicago pretty quickly. Within moments, I realized all the faces were familiar, save for one. She was an attractive and extroverted woman with long brown hair, caramel skin, and freckles who appeared to know everyone in our group except me. My interest was piqued. I certainly wanted to get to know this woman better, starting with her name—Dr. Shawn Smith. I asked if I could get her a glass of wine, and she decided to go with me to the beverage line. I was thrilled to have a few more-private moments with this intriguing woman, although we didn't break off from our friends for long. A few minutes later, when she told me she was a pediatrics resident at UChicago, I was so visibly shocked that my friends chimed in, assuring me it was true. There were so few residents of color at UChicago's hospitals and clinics that I thought I'd met everyone, no matter their specialty. Clearly I was wrong. As fate would have it, due to the complexity of rotation schedules and UChicago locations, Dr. Smith and I simply hadn't crossed paths until this moment, two-thousand miles away from our medical campus. After I picked my jaw up from the floor, I managed to play it cool for the rest of the reception. However, as soon as the evening ended, I regrouped with my boys to get the scoop on Dr. Smith, and the reports were all good. I was enticed.

The conference kept me busy for the next few days, although we did have a scheduled half-day respite. That morning, a group of my friends and I decided to go to the beach for some chill time. It was a hot but breezy day, and the beach was fairly crowded. My friends were no doubt looking forward to some sunbathing and a dip in the Pacific's refreshing waters, but I had my own agenda: spending some time with Dr. Smith. Not wanting to come on too strong, I held back for a minute, but eventually I found my way to a towel alongside her, then pleasantly distracted her from her book with some conversation and a little flirting. She indulged my curiosity, drawing me in further with her beautiful smile as we puzzled through the mystery of our long-uncrossed paths. Even at this early meeting, it crossed my mind that the kind, thoughtful, and highly intellectual physician next to me had many of the attributes I wanted in a partner, although I really wasn't sure if she was feeling me. Even still, I figured I had a chance with this alluring young doctor as long as I didn't mess things up by making some juvenile misstep. My time with her flew by, then suddenly it was time to wrap things up and head back to the conference for our afternoon sessions. To commemorate our time together, the group and I took some pictures before leaving the beach behind.

I had a few things on my mind as I returned to Chicago. With less than a year left, my residency training was almost complete, and I needed to decide if I wanted to stay in Chicago (hopefully as an attending) or pursue positions elsewhere. I would soon be applying to business schools both inside and outside of Chicago, a process that would require time, focus, and attention on top of the prep work I needed to do for the last of my residency exams. Additionally, my beloved fraternity had asked me to chair a national committee focused on mentoring; I'd been compelled to accept the role as a way of giving back at least a portion of the support I'd been afforded over the years. On top of all that, I now needed to reprioritize dating, especially if I wanted to get to know Dr. Smith better.

Over the next few months, I was on the lookout for Dr. Smith. I wanted to be subtle with my continuing interest and possibly even engineer some "accidental," casual moments together during breaks or shift changes. That did *not* work out very well—our workplaces were nothing like the TV show *Grey's Anatomy*, where residents hung out in the basement after sneaking away from their wards. No matter how hard I tried to orchestrate an encounter, Dr. Smith remained elusive. Thankfully, because I could always count on my boys, one day I received a text from John with an important heads-up: Dr. Smith was currently rotating in the pediatric ER. Since I was on shift in the adjoining adult ER, I made an excuse to hightail it over there for some eye contact and a quick conversation. The pediatric ER was small, and the attending on shift that evening was Dr. Gail Allen—the only Black EM attending in pediatrics at UChicago at that time—who took notice of us as we talked. She knew all the residents of color well, and I'm pretty sure she saw some sparks between me and Dr. Smith.

After that first in-hospital conversation, I made sure I had Dr.

Smith's phone number so we could keep in touch. I found reasons to walk through the pediatric ER to see if she was around or steal glances of her during her shifts, and I even offered to help her if she ever needed to perform an unfamiliar EM procedure. Well, never once did Dr. Smith need my help during her rotation, and by all accounts she performed her job brilliantly. As a graduate of both Clark Atlanta University and Boston University School of Medicine, she was very astute and always on top of her game clinically.

Our "adjoining" rotations lasted for a few weeks, but afterward our schedules diverged once again. As was typical for EM residents, my next rotation moved me to another hospital affiliated with my residency program, and Dr. Smith rotated into the pediatric intensive care unit. This meant a few more months went by before our first official date. Yet there was a Divine hand at work here, one that was silently fostering patience so our relationship could unfold. Although the demands of our respective residencies and career aspirations didn't leave a lot of time for dating, it didn't take us long to realize we had something special together. In time, our sporadic dates transformed into a healthy relationship. Over the next few years, that relationship grew into a partnership, one filled with memorable travel moments, including a 2007 trip to Sydney. By the end of that summer, I'd bought a ring with the hope that Dr. Shawn Smith would accept me as her fiancé. Observing tradition, I then hopped onto a flight to Detroit to ask her dad for permission to marry his daughter. He graciously gave me that permission, and a few days later, when Shawn said yes to my proposal, I was a man overjoyed. Our engagement lasted about a year, and on August 30th, 2008, four years after we'd first met, Dr. Shawn Smith did me the honor of making me her husband. Thirteen years (and counting) since our wedding day, and we're now the proud parents of two bright, energetic, and competitive sons.

Looking back on July 31, 2004, I know it was God who, in a single day, used the tears I shed at Kenny's funeral to water a new seed, one that His hand planted the moment I met Shawn. My mind and heart that day were refocused on the one thing in life that mattered the most, the one thing that would endure over all else: love.

CHAPTER 12

Preparing for Leadership

ONE OF THE GREATEST PRIVILEGES OF MY LIFE HAS BEEN TO CARE FOR patients in the emergency room, where many face the most vulnerable moments of their lives. By its very nature, the ER is a volatile, unpredictable place, and EM doctors must challenge their assumptions, lead treatment-teams through highly charged emotional moments, and even push their own physical limits fairly often. Unfortunately, diseases don't care how taxing an EM physician's shift has been or how many patients they treated that day, and car accidents, perpetrators of violence, and heart attacks or strokes do not wreak their havoc on a regular schedule. The goal of every doctor in every ER is to save (or improve) patient lives, and to do this, EM physicians must assume leadership every day, and not just in terms of medical knowledge. They must inject calmness, grace, and even patience into chaotic situations where many factors beyond their control are at work. In other words, as Dr. LaSalle Leffall taught me at Howard, "equanimity under duress" must win the day, every day.

I was first drawn to the possibility of service beyond clinical care during my years at Howard. As a resident of DC and student in the

College of Medicine, I saw physician-leaders making large-scale impacts through their efforts in research, education, business, public health, organized medicine, and policy. Like so many who'd walked the halls of Howard, these legends in healthcare pioneered new treatments, challenged entrenched assumptions, and blazed new trails in outreach—and they did it all while living in a society that didn't always embrace their efforts, passions, and intellects. Their successes opened my mind to an even higher level of physician-service than I'd ever envisioned. Through their tireless pursuits, so many of Howard's physician-leaders had built legacies, and I sometimes wondered if I could create impact enough during my career to be counted among them.

I was having lunch one day in the HUH cafeteria with a group of classmates, and we began discussing the legacies of Howard physicians and contemplating the directions and steps needed for creating legacies of our own. We considered whether enrolling in other graduate-level programs after our four years of medical school would indeed broaden our perspectives and open doors for us down the road. We certainly didn't have all the answers, but in that moment a new goal was planted in my mind: after I earned my MD, and after I finished my residency training, I would enroll in business school. I wanted to pursue management or leadership positions in those segments of the healthcare industry that influence the quality of care for all Americans. When I discussed the idea with HUH's chief financial officer, he thought supplementing my education with an MBA was a great idea. Later, when it came time for me to apply to residencies, he encouraged me to consider training in Chicago because the city was home to major hospitals, healthcare associations, and excellent business schools alike.

When I Matched at UChicago and moved to the Midwest, the

opportunities before me were limited only by my own vision, yet I couldn't possibly have anticipated how my interests in leadership, public health, and politics would shape my UChicago years. About six months into my first year of residency, I heard my first call to service as a physician-activist when I was attending my program's weekly departmental meeting. Most of these meetings were led by UChicago faculty, but once per month my program hosted a guest speaker, usually someone of regional or national prominence. One cold and wintery day, Dr. Susan Nedza was our guest speaker. A nationally known EM specialist, Dr. Nedza was on the board of the American College of Emergency Physicians (ACEP) and had a long history of leadership at the state and national levels. During her presentation, she addressed the many intersections between EM care, health policy, politics, and organized medicine. I was fascinated. When, at the end of her talk, she told us about the ACEP's annual spring Leadership and Advocacy Conference in DC, I intuitively knew I needed to be there.

Immediately following the meeting, I joined my program director, Dr. David Howes, in a conversation with Dr. Nedza. I asked Dr. Howes if he would support my attending the conference. As a prolific recruiter of top talent for UChicago's EM training program, and as an educator who thrived on steering residents toward leadership roles, Dr. Howes was quick to reply with a resounding yes. Just as he did so, Dr. Nedza said she would be delighted to take me under her wing and introduce me to her contacts and colleagues at the conference.

When I saw DC from the air, a pang of nostalgia hit me as I arrived in the city where I'd created so many memories. The skyline of our capital was familiar, yet the reason for my return was brand new: I would be joining the legions of Americans who actively engaged their representative government. However, at the conference, I was disappointed (although not terribly surprised) at the lack of racial and ethnic diversity among attendees—with only a handful of people of color like me in the room, we stood out. Similarly, with over two hundred physicians present, I was amazed when I learned that fewer than a dozen were residents. Since I was among these few on both counts, I certainly had the chance to shine, and I dived in wholeheartedly.

With Dr. Nedza supporting me throughout the conference, I had the good fortune of meeting and getting to know some of the country's most influential EM leaders. They lost no time in enlightening me about the ways healthcare advocates could influence the political system, and they opened my eyes to the many possibilities for physicians outside of clinical-care settings. This was a major turning point in my leadership development: I could help individuals in the ER, *and* I could have a hand in shaping state and/or national healthcare policies, so I eagerly signed up for the advocate-training sessions being offered. My instructors covered tips on interacting with media, the basic dos and don'ts of advocacy, and—most invaluably—the fundamentals of staying on message.

When the time came to visit Capitol Hill on the last day of the conference, I felt I had a solid, if broad, understanding of advocacy as an art—and as a tool. I had already, if briefly, bonded with many of the physician-leaders on the ACEP's Illinois delegation, and now, as we met with Congresspeople and their staffs, we had plenty of information to impart. Members of our delegation came from all corners of Illinois, and we represented a panoramic picture of our state's healthcare landscape, from urban hospitals with academic medical centers to rural hospitals. Although I was the youngest in our group, as a flight physician who'd transported patients from all over northern Illinois to UChicago, I had unique information to contribute. I illustrated the regional differences in healthcare accessibility by sharing the stories of transport patients who didn't have specialized, often lifesaving, medical services available in their communities. From there, our delegation's senior members explained how these divides were the consequence of legislative action (or inaction) and policies that reinforced inequity. When the delegation and I saw how deeply our messages resonated with Illinois' Congresspeople, we instantly knew we would be working together again.

Not long after I returned from DC, the Illinois College of Emergency Physicians (ICEP), which was headed by many of the doctors I'd met at the ACEP conference, asked me to join them in their advocacy work, which included periodically traveling to Springfield (the capital of Illinois) for meetings. I heartily agreed, and soon I was among the state's few resident physicians who were engaged in the politics of healthcare. As an ICEP advocate, I called attention to the high number of Illinoisans who didn't have health insurance and/or primary-care physicians. I educated our state legislature about the many ways that poverty could beget poor health, and I brought to the fore the many disparities I saw daily in the ER.

Even though my work as an ICEP advocate was rewarding, I still had a strong interest in working on the national level. In late 2003, that interest was met when I was fortunate enough to be appointed by the ACEP's president to its Federal Government Affairs Committee; at the same time, I also began serving on the board of the National Emergency Medicine Political Action Committee (NEMPAC). Now working at the national level, I reviewed, at regular intervals, ACEP-staff-prepared analyses of all proposed healthcare bills. As those bills then moved through Congress, I paid special attention to how they could affect emergency medicine and care. I learned about the ways special-interest groups, including those in various medical specialties, raised monies enough to ensure access to both sides of the aisle as they pushed their agendas forward. I saw how dissimilar organizations and industries could find common ground when they had shared interests on bills. Just from being in the room, I formed an early understanding of DC's legislative processes, including the necessity of balancing my visits to Capitol Hill with the prompt mobilization of constituents who were often needed to ensure a bill made it to the floor. Additionally, I continued to share patient stories illustrative of systemic healthcare issues, and I recommended specific healthcare-forward actions for our legislators to take.

Parallel to my work with the ACEP, I took on a leadership role within the Emergency Medicine Residents' Association (EMRA), a national organization. With a strong year of organized medicine experience through the ACEP under my belt, when the EMRA held its 2004 board of directors' election, I decided to run for the ACEP representative role. The EMRA board member who held this position attended all ACEP board meetings and was responsible for liaising between the ACEP and EMRA boards. To win, I had to present a credible case to the EMRA membership and convince them I was the best candidate. I was uncertain of the outcome, but when the votes were tallied, it was clear the membership agreed that I should serve in the role. For two years, I worked with some of the brightest EM resident physicians in the country. Plus, in taking this position I, however unexpectedly, served in another way too: as a graduating resident, I bridged the generational divide between the two organizations, as ACEP members tended to be in mid-career while EMRA members were only beginning theirs. However, no matter which of the two organizations a physician belonged to, each of us was ambitious and in search of ways to change our respective worlds.

Serving as the EMRA representative to ACEP's board was a very rewarding but heavy task, especially as I was still a resident during the first year of my term. My board position brought me all around the country (and especially to ACEP headquarters in Dallas), so I often had to juggle my rotations to accommodate these trips. By the time I took the position, Dr. Nedza had rotated off the ACEP's board and moved onto an executive role at the US Department of Health and Human Services, but I had already established good working relationships with a number of current board members, many of whom were at the pinnacles of their careers, and they shared their knowledge with me freely while making me feel at home. With their help, I became a quick study on the politics of emergency medicine, the organization itself, and the physicians we served. Our pre-meeting binders were often three inches thick and had vast amounts of information to digest, but it was worth it because I could see the changes our work effected. Almost as importantly, the relationships I formed with ACEP leaders laid the groundwork for lifelong colleagueships—and friendships— with some of the best minds in the specialty. When one of our board meetings was held in the Mexican city of Manzanillo (on the country's west coast), I went on my first deep-sea fishing trip and discovered a fishing buddy in board chairman Dr. John Bibb. For several years afterward, I joined John and his club of senior physicians for chartered tuna-fishing trips along the California coast, which provided periodic respites from the responsibilities we carried as advocates and emergency physicians.

Unlike college, medical school, and my residency, the chain of events that brought me to leadership was not the result of any path I had planned. As a very young man, I had taken on limited leadership roles in both my native city and at Xavier, but I had never truly aspired to politics, medical or otherwise. Others saw the potential for leadership in me even when I didn't see it myself, and I was blessed with many mentors, colleagues, and friends who had experience in organized medicine, public health, and advocacy. I remain deeply grateful to both Dr. Howes and Dr. Nedza for giving me my first shot at real leadership so early in my career.

For the rest of my residency, throughout my time in business school, and during my early attending years, I continued my leadership and service to the ACEP and NEMPAC; I stepped down only when, to avoid any conflict of interest, I accepted my first executive role with the Federal government. As my career advanced, I held C-suite roles in both the public and private sectors, and I served on various non-profit boards. In 2018, it was truly humbling to accept an invitation to join Xavier University of Louisiana's board of trustees. All in all, no matter which organization I was working with, I was always able to be of service in a way that advanced the health or well-being of others, and I will be forever grateful to the larger village that invested in me over the years.

CHAPTER 13

Vignettes from the ER

THE LAST FEW MONTHS OF MY RESIDENCY WERE A JUGGLING ACT LIKE no other. Studying for the last of my residency exams, preparing for graduation, working in the ER, applying to and interviewing at business schools, and keeping on top of my advocacy work meant that I barely had a moment to myself during the earlier months of 2005.

My plan was to pursue my MBA in a full-time program while also working part-time as an EM physician, which meant I needed to find a graduate program that would support me not just as a student, but as a working professional with real responsibilities to patients. I tapped my network for advice and recommendations, applied to four schools, and interviewed at two or three of them. By the time the dust had settled, I had been accepted to two of the world's most prestigious business schools: UChicago's Booth School of Business (then named the Graduate School of Business) and Harvard Business School in Massachusetts. I hadn't necessarily been committed to staying in Chicago, but with a local, world-class program practically in my backyard, I decided the Graduate School of Business was right for me.

Once I knew I wasn't moving, I needed to discover the best area hospital at which to start my career as a residency-trained EM specialist. After being an underpaid resident for the last three years, the prospect of earning a healthy paycheck was certainly appealing, and I knew the job market for EM physicians with my qualifications was fairly hot. I started my job search by connecting with alumni of my residency program. They pointed me toward any number of openings, and I interviewed at three or four EM practices. Each position was attractive in its own way, even though the overall process reminded me of buying a used car: every hospital showed its absolute best during the brief test drive, yet I couldn't truly tell what was under the hood. I had many questions needing answers, answers that I couldn't possibly get without on-the-ground experience at any given hospital: When I found myself in a bind and in need of emergent help from another specialist, how quickly would my pages be answered with in-person assistance? How did their ER *really* function at 2:00 a.m.? Did the doctors and administrators *truly* care about their patients, or did they just view those in need of medical care as revenue? With the limited information available to me, I had to make a decision—then live with the outcome.

After much contemplation, just like anyone starting their first professional job, I took a leap of faith and picked the position that seemed best for me. I joined an EM group that staffed the emergency department at Ingalls Memorial Hospital (which is today UChicago Medicine Ingalls Memorial) in Harvey, a suburb just south of Chicago. Ingalls was an independent community hospital in a working-class community of color. The group I chose was an exciting practice to join as I knew I'd be welcomed by both colleagues and the community itself. However, like most practices and hospitals, there were few Black, male physicians on staff, and I was the only one in the group. The staff of Ingalls itself had a similar make up; for a Black man, he was exponentially more likely to be a member of the environmental services team than a physician. At the same time, though, I was confident that I could better my skills and increase my scope at Ingalls, particularly as their emergency department was an early adopter of electronic health records (EHRs). The emerging technology integrated lab results, radiology interpretations, and physician orders into e-records that streamlined patient care, and the ED was so cutting edge that we were the only department at Ingalls using it. Just like my clerkship at Howard's Telehealth Science and Advanced Technology Center, this use of EHRs was ahead of its time—several more years would pass before EHRs were universally adopted in the US. (Later in my journey, when the government invested billions of dollars in EHR programs, I helped catalyze the movement toward EHR adoption. Additionally, and very importantly for me, the heads of my practice supported my MBA pursuit, were willing and able to take me on as a part-time attending, and helped ensure that my clinical schedule worked around my class schedule. I remain grateful to the physician group led by Dr. Saif Nazir for embracing me and accommodating my educational journey through business school.

Like anyone starting their first professional job, the first two or three months were a time of transition. Although I was embraced by most of the ED's nurses, I could tell that I needed to prove myself to the more-senior ones. Looking back, I can't say I blame them: I was a young, eager doctor fresh out of residency who wore a shirt and tie (rather than scrubs) to work, while the seasoned nurses were often old enough to be my mother and had decades of clinical experience. It took a little charming and a whole lot of outstanding patient care, but soon enough, I managed to win them over. As is essential for any optimally functioning ED, we established a mutual trust and respect that allowed us to give one-hundred-and-ten percent to providing incredible, seamless care for the patients we served.

As an attending, providing medical care in the ER is a rollercoaster ride of triumphs and losses connected by stretches of routine cases and mundane presentations. I've sutured lacerations, treated upper respiratory infections, and diagnosed back pain more times than I could ever count, but some patient-care stories remain vivid in my memory, whether I was working at Ingalls or at the other hospitals I moved on to. Over the years, my mind has become laden with stories that have softened my heart or tested my emotional resilience. As if someone were whispering in my ear, I can still hear ghosts of my own thoughts from moments when I was scrambling to diagnose the root of idiopathic symptoms or faced presentations so graphic and disturbing that I'll never be able to unsee them. From Illinois to Georgia to Indiana, I did my best for all of my patients. What follows is a sampling of my most memorable ER encounters.

ON THE FOURTH OF JULY

Working the overnight shift during a holiday wasn't ever a walk in the park, but one Fourth of July at Ingalls still haunts me. The night was relatively quiet until we received a frantic radio call from an EMT unit: a child had been shot.

The EMTs told us they were three minutes out. We were given a few other details, then we rushed to prepare our trauma room for a pediatric resuscitation. With the essentials in place, I went to the trauma bay door. I expected the child to be brought to us like most other acute trauma victims: strapped to a backboard, neck wrapped in a cervical collar, and IV lines set up. Not this time. When the ambulance's doors opened, a paramedic was holding a limp, four-year-old child in her arms. She rushed the unconscious boy to the trauma room's bed, placing him gently across it. The surgical lights above illuminated the devastation. A single bullet had entered one side of his head and exited through the other, leaving a small amount of brain matter in his hair.

This young boy had been in the backseat of his parents' car, outside of a store, when gunfire erupted. My team and I suppressed our horror and kept our heads clear as we cared for our young patient. Standing at the head of the bed, I intubated him with an emergency breathing tube. We made sure he had no other injuries, placed IVs, and started him on medications to reduce swelling in the brain. As soon as I was able, I called one of our pediatric trauma centers to have him transported by helicopter to a facility offering neurosurgical care. The team and I had done all we could, but it was unclear whether our patient, a child so young he was barely out of diapers, would survive.

After preparing the boy for the inbound flight team, I stepped out of the ER to speak with his mom. I tried to offer her hope while not downplaying the odds. Assuring her that her son was receiving the best care possible, I told her we were in a minute-by-minute situation that would hopefully progress to hour-by-hour improvement, then day-by-day. Trying to imagine her pain and fear, I held her in my arms as she cried. I empathized with her deeply. This case tested and strengthened the emotional limits of our team. After the child had been airlifted, we allowed ourselves a moment so our feelings could decompress, but then we built another emotional wall to prepare us for the next emergency.

During the following winter, I was walking through a short hallway that connected the fast-track section of the ED to its main room. In mid-stride I was stopped by a woman entering the stairwell. She called out, "Hey doctor, do you remember me?" I shook my head—she and the child beside her were bundled up in their coats and hats, unrecognizable under the layers. "You came to speak to me the night my son was shot—and here he is!" She pulled back the hood of the boy's coat and pulled off his hat. "Thank you so much." There stood my young patient, with a slightly crooked smile and joy in his eyes. I gave him a big hug, and his mom let me take a selfie with him. The child was alive and walking, and all I could think about was the grace of God.

SON OF THE CONFEDERACY

At one point in my career, I held a federal appointment with regional-oversight responsibilities, so I traveled to Georgia a few times each month to see patients. One sweltering summer day, an unresponsive twelve-year-old boy was pulled from a neighborhood swimming pool. Because every second counted, the paramedics had employed a scoop-and-run strategy; they'd initiated CPR and immediately loaded the patient into the ambulance, rather than using more advanced, more time-consuming, in-the-field strategies. When we received the call, we prepared our resuscitation room for the boy's arrival, knowing that this would be a difficult case. When the EMTs brought the child in, one member of our team took over chest compressions as the rest of us removed his wet clothes. His heart wasn't beating on its own, and his skin was bluish from oxygen deprivation. His torso was still warm, though—a single, hopeful sign. I cleared the vomit from his mouth and placed a breathing tube emergently into his airway; meanwhile, the team dried his skin and placed two defibrillator pads on his chest.

We continued chest compressions, with one of us supplying a periodic breath into his lungs through the endotracheal tube. The monitor showed that our patient's heart was in ventricular fibrillation, a life-threatening arrhythmia that is treated by electrical shock. We charged the defibrillator, and when it was full we yelled, "I'm clear, you're clear, everyone's clear. Shocking now." We administered two more rounds of medications, including epinephrine, atropine, and a sodium bicarbonate dose. Yet the monitor was flatline, indicating asystole. As the team continued CPR, I left the room to find the child's parents. Whenever possible, I would bring the parents into the room during a juvenile resuscitation, even if only to hold their child in the last moments of life.

About ten yards away, just outside the ambulance-bay entrance, I found the boy's father. He was clearly distraught, yet I immediately questioned my ability to connect with him—his tank top revealed that his arms were tattooed with Confederate flags and other white-supremacy symbols. I wondered if—as had happened before—he would request a doctor whose skin matched his own. Worse, if his son died, would there be trouble for me in the parking lot after my shift?

From growing up in the South, I'd always been familiar with the rationale that the Confederate flag is a symbol of heritage. Yet I also knew how I'd been treated by the guys at my high school who'd proudly displayed this flag on their cars, jackets, or lockers, so I had to force myself not to assume that this father wasn't an adult version of the same. In history lessons and discussions at home, I came to understand how pro-Confederacy monuments had been erected across the South in the first half of the twentieth century as enduring testaments to hatred, white supremacy, and slavery. Even outside the courthouse in my hometown, throughout my entire childhood, the Stars and Bars were proudly flown above a monument to Confederate generals. With the father's symbols of hate and oppression on full display, I was challenged to connect with him personally, as individual connection was at the heart of who I was as a physician.

No matter my feelings about this father's tattoos or his beliefs, I still had a duty to both him and his son. Aware of my bias, I approached the man and invited him inside the hospital. He looked at me with hope in his eyes. As we walked down the hall together, I explained the scene he would see in the resuscitation room, and I assured him we were doing everything we could to save his son. Once in the room, as I turned my attention back to my patient, the teary-eyed father held his son's foot tenderly and, a few minutes later, took the boy's right hand in his.

After a few additional minutes of CPR, we paused to check the boy's pulse and interpret his heart rhythm on the monitor. Surprisingly, the monitor showed a sinus tachycardia, and we could feel a strong pulse in his arm; hope was in the air. We knew the child wasn't out of the woods yet—brain damage or injury to other organs were still real possibilities—but he had a chance. His father was grateful for our efforts to save his son, and I led him and the team in a brief prayer. A few moments later, the transport team arrived and flew our young patient to a hospital offering pediatric critical care.

As I heard the helicopter flying away, I was reminded that children shouldn't be faulted for the decisions and attitudes of their parents. None of us have control over the circumstances we're born into; until we're adults, we don't have autonomy enough to truly make choices for ourselves. And while I will never know, perhaps this father's views were different from what I believed them to be or had evolved after he'd received his tattoos. Regardless, it's my duty to provide treatment and care to those in crisis, even when it means casting aside my own fears, misgivings, or assumptions. Especially in the ER, patients and their families always come first.

A SPLIT-SECOND DECISION

One cold morning at an Indiana hospital, as I arrived for my 6:00 a.m. shift, I noticed the ER was unusually quiet—no gurneys in the hallway or patients awaiting beds. Just as I sat down to prepare for our sign-out protocols (i.e., the process of transferring patients to an attending who's starting their shift), the radio sounded with an alert. A trauma patient was coming in, and the estimated time of arrival was "pulling up in the back now."

The patient had been shot in the head. I sprang into action and met the paramedics as they rushed him into the trauma room. They relayed his vitals, noting that he had gone into cardiac arrest just before arrival. No further details were available, but it was easy to see that the patient was bleeding heavily, his face and scalp swelling dangerously.

The injury from the bullet was devastating, but even more urgent was the blood filling the man's mouth. On the ride to the ER, the paramedics had placed a double-lumen tube into his throat to ventilate his lungs, but it wasn't working well. The source of the blood in the lungs, mouth, and throat didn't seem connected to the cranial bullet wound, but whatever the cause, I needed to remove the current tube and instead insert a single-lumen tube that—when placed precisely inside his windpipe—would protect the man from drowning in his own blood. But faster than we could move, his heart rate dropped, putting him in cardiac arrest again.

The team began CPR as I removed the old tube and began suctioning blood from the man's mouth. I'd performed this type of siphoning before, but unlike in the past, the suction couldn't keep pace with the bleeding, and I had to slow the hemorrhaging by packing part of the mouth with sterile gauze. With the bleeding somewhat under control, I inserted a laryngoscope into the man's mouth and down to the back of the airway. Even though my instrument had a bright light at its tip, the normal structures of the throat didn't come into view—all I saw was bloody, macerated tissue. I examined further; the bullet, on its path of destruction, had cut down through the brain and into the throat, likely lodging down in the chest. Clearing and securing his airway was emergent, yet now, between the copious amount of blood and the tissue damage itself, I knew that no fiberoptic camera, no matter how advanced, could aid me in placing the lumen tube.

Aghast at the discovery and with CPR in progress, inside of a split second, I changed plans. "I need an eleven-blade, scalpel, and some ChloraPrep!" I yelled. The team knew what this meant: I needed to create a surgical airway, a last-resort procedure that EM physicians train for but rarely have to perform. The nurse across from me muttered, "I've never seen one of these before," as I splashed some ChloraPrep on the patient's neck to sterilize the area. I looked up for an instant and saw six pairs of eyes watching intensely. If I successfully created the airway, he might have a remote chance of surviving; if I missed, so many cards were stacked against him that he would certainly die. I didn't have time for a mental, ethical argument about the prospective quality of my patient's life if he survived. Opening an airway was paramount, and that's where I placed my focus and energy.

I gave my team the sign to briefly pause chest compressions. With confidence and precision, I made a one-centimeter, vertical incision into the cricothyroid area (just below the larynx), exposing the underlying membrane. A second one-centimeter incision, this one internal and horizontal, granted me access to the windpipe. I used my scalpel's handle to hold the surgically created pathway open, even as I inserted a breathing tube with my other hand. The procedure took only seven seconds, and the instant I got the breathing tube positioned and taped in place along the neck, I jumped back so the team could resume chest compressions.

Almost immediately, the monitors showed increased oxygen in the lungs. One or two minutes later, the patient's pulse returned and was strong. With his vitals stabilized, a flight team soon came to transfer our patient to a Level-One trauma center for further care.

THE OBSTETRIC EMERGENCY

I was in my second year as an attending when one morning, a little before seven o'clock, a call came over the radio: an ambulance with a woman in active labor (and pushing) was five minutes away. As I called out to the staff to prep for her arrival, a few of the nurses gave me the side-eye because it was as if obstetric emergencies had been following me over the last few months—laboring mothers, or pregnant women having seizures, often came in just after the start of my 6:00 a.m. shift. I called upstairs to obstetrics to give the ob-gyn attending a heads-up. Because nurses and other non-EM staff typically changed shifts at 7:00 a.m., which was now only a few minutes away, there couldn't have been a more inconvenient time for an incoming delivery.

Under my white coat, I was dressed well in khaki cargo pants, a crisply pressed blue shirt, and a red tie, with red-turtle cufflinks to complete my outfit. The nurses sometimes chided me about my attire, but dressing well helped me bring my A-game to work every day. In anticipation of possibly delivering a baby, I threw on fluid-resistant shoe covers and a sterile surgical gown. As I was slipping on a pair of latex gloves, the nurses brought a radiant warmer for infants into the resuscitation room as a precaution. Unless the baby's head was crowning, our standard practice for labor cases was to send mom upstairs so her child could be delivered in the maternity ward. Our mantra was, "Never let the wheels on the cart stop moving," which meant, in this case, that time in the ER for a healthy, non-critical, laboring mother should be as brief as possible, as the safest place for birthing is always the labor and delivery ward.

We heard the ambulance's siren as it pulled into the bay. The noise stopped as the driver cut the engine, but the wailing had only been masking the pain-filled moans of a woman in labor. The EMTs rolled her through the hall and into the resuscitation room. With my sterile hands clasped in front of me, I waited at the door of the room for my patient, knowing the EMTs were just around the corner. As she entered the room and we pulled the curtain, the mother's pregnant abdomen indicated that she was in her third trimester, and I took a quick look under her sheet to see if the baby was presenting. My hope was that all our preparation had magically obviated the need for an ER delivery. I was wrong. As I examined my patient, I immediately discovered a blue-tinged foot and an umbilical cord in the vaginal canal.

Typically, in the last few weeks of pregnancy, a fetus turns in the mother's womb and positions itself for a headfirst delivery. If a fetus doesn't turn, the birth is breech, and this can be extremely dangerous.

While I had delivered many babies before, I'd never delivered one in the breech position. But more importantly in this case, the umbilical cord (which supplies oxygenated blood and nutrients to the baby) was stuck in the vagina; as the mother preceded with her labor and the baby continued through the vaginal canal, the baby would compress the umbilical cord, thus cutting off his own blood-oxygen. Fetal distress was all-but guaranteed, and there was even a real chance that the baby could die.

I had to act decisively. First and foremost, with my gloved, sterile hand, I reached into the patient's vagina and elevated the baby's foot, ensuring continued blood flow through the umbilical cord. I instructed our charge nurse to call up to the operating room and have a room cleared for an emergency C-section delivery. I then climbed on top of the patient's gurney, my hand still elevating the baby's foot, and instructed the team to roll us out of the emergency department, into an elevator, and up to the operating room.

The ER's unit secretary had notified the ob-gyn attending to meet us in the operating room. Until then, it was crucial that I keep my hand where it was for the sake of both mother and baby. I could hardly imagine the thoughts going through the mother's head as she felt contraction after contraction and moaned in pain and fear. I tried to reassure her—as long as the baby's foot wasn't pressing on the umbilical cord, she and her child were out of immediate danger.

About five minutes after arriving in the operating room, a member of the ob-gyn team took over for me. Freed from my position, I was able to wash up and return to the ED—this time walking instead of riding. The ER team was impressed; I'd potentially saved the child's life, sure, but somehow the bigger deal was my having kept my shirt, tie, and pants clean through the chaos. I laughed. I'd managed to stay clean this time, but it was still early in my shift—it was yet to be seen what the rest of the day would bring.

Later in the day, I was able to steal a moment and head up to the maternity ward to check on the situation. The baby, born a few weeks premature, had been placed in the neonatal intensive care unit and was doing well. The mother was okay, too.

For each of these cases, there are a thousand other patients who I've had the privilege of caring for over the years. Most were first-time encounters for urgent and emergent concerns, and extending respect and empathy is always among the first of the instruments in my medical bag. Each patient interaction has been an opportunity to understand, to comfort, and to better lives. After my patients leave the ED, I don't always learn the endings of their stories, but I know I've made a difference, no matter how mundane or severe their needs were when they came in. Yet, like most EM physicians, I have borne witness to unimaginable nightmares through my work, but I have also been inspired by the battles so many of my patients have won; the graceful longevity and wisdom I see in so many of my senior patients reminds me of the incredible privilege I have in being a physician.

CHAPTER 14

From Physician to C-Suite

PROVIDING DIRECT CARE TO PATIENTS IN THE ER WAS MY WAY OF CARing for those in need at the individual level, yet I yearned to impact healthcare at a larger scale, one that I couldn't realize by seeing patients at their bedsides. I would need to start down a new trail if I were to achieve my dreams. But after a decade and a half of having my course laid out for me—four years of college, four years of medical school, three years of residency, four years as a practicing EM physician including two years of business school—the path for elevating my healthcare impact was broad and uncharted. I had specific areas of interest on which I was eager to focus my energy and efforts, such as addressing healthcare disparities and broadening access to affordable healthcare, but there was no playbook with step-by-step instructions outlining the right moves, and the healthcare industry itself was evolving at a rapid pace. At this time in the 2000s, a great national discussion about the future of American healthcare was gaining real momentum (This discussion led to the 2010 Affordable Care Act, a.k.a Obamacare.), yet at this time, the reality of a nationwide, public-buy-in, health-insurance system was not a certain outcome. But what was clear was that the next move, with all its inherent risks, was on me. To successfully maneuver my career to the next level meant taking careful inventory of my strengths, past experiences, and my own areas for growth. Essentially, I had to make myself deeply vulnerable in a way I hadn't done since I'd started applying to medical schools some ten years earlier.

I tapped my network asking for advice and perspective as I was exploring both private- and public-service opportunities. I wanted to find a position where my passion for service to others and my years of physicianship intersected with shaping health outcomes on a regional, state, or even national level. Colleagues and friends from ACEP and my alumni networks gave me some tips on accessing the private sector, and they also advised me on the unique value of public service at the Federal level, especially during a time when transformative changes in policy were eminently possible. Speaking from their own respective experience in federal service, my advisors fertilized my potential for moving into public health and policy, and I trusted that they were giving me the right advice at the right time in my journey.

Once I better understood the landscape of opportunities, I began connecting with specialized employment agencies and interviewing for executive roles that aligned strongly with my interests. This approach offered no guarantee of employment, but it certainly gave me plenty of chances to deliver my elevator pitch about my career and professional aspirations. I gave this pitch at four interviews, but ultimately it seemed I was getting nowhere fast.

When the right opportunity did come, it came from one of my many mentors. Once again, the very people who had shaped my journey were looking out for me as I transitioned into the next part of my career, and I landed my first executive job as the chief medical officer for the Centers for Medicare and Medicaid Services (CMS), an operating division of the US Department of Health and Human Services. While this position wasn't exactly what I had in mind for myself post-business school, it was an excellent opportunity for an early-career physician-executive, and it offered me unprecedented access to the local and regional healthcare infrastructure. Even better, the Chicago regional office (unlike the locations of some other local Federal buildings) was in the city's central business district, known as the Loop, and it was just steps from Michigan Avenue—home of Chicago's Magnificent Mile. It was near the headquarters of many influential healthcare organizations: ACGME, the American Hospital Association, the American Medical Association, the Blue Cross and Blue Shield Association, the Health Care Service Corporation, and the Illinois State Medical Society. They were all within a mile; geographically, I was in an excellent place to start my career as a physician-executive.

I began at CMS in the summer of 2009. CMS is the US' largest payer of healthcare services, and as chief medical officer I had oversight responsibility for Illinois, Indiana, Michigan, Minnesota, Ohio, and Wisconsin. At the time, our region (designated as Region 5) encompassed the second-largest population of Medicare beneficiaries and the third-largest population of Medicaid beneficiaries in the country. Among other things, this meant that I was actively working for the best interests of many of the most vulnerable members of our society each day. Moreover, because CMS is also a regulatory agency, it plays a critical role in defining the quality and safety guidelines for healthcare given by its contracted providers, and—because most providers who accept Medicare/Medicaid also accept other insurances alongside direct-pay from the uninsured—these regulations impact nearly everyone in the country. Just by doing my job, I had a hand in improving healthcare for hundreds of millions of Americans.

Although my responsibilities as chief medical officer were broad, my most important role was being the key clinician who liaised between CMS and all healthcare providers in the region. When we had bright spots of success with our providers and community organizations, I was often able, with the agency's go-ahead, to lift up that great work publicly. Keeping CMS in the public eye at this time was especially important since we were spearheading the acceleration of a more value-driven healthcare system alongside a comprehensive, rapid adoption of new technology. Hospitals, nursing homes, transplant centers, testing labs, home-health and durable-equipment suppliers, and others all passed through my office. As a part of keeping all entities informed, it was my job to translate complex, wordy, and jargon-filled regulations into everyday language that was understandable for healthcare providers and patients alike. This tedious (but important and meaningful) work often left me squinting by the end of the day, but I was glad to do my part in making healthcare policy understandable to the public.

In contrast to my work as a "translator," the most exciting part of the job for me was giving regular feedback to the government, especially when I could offer real, on-the-ground insights on programs and rules that we at CMS may have gotten wrong or needed to update. For example, CMS once sought to curtail safety problems associated with patient sedation during endoscopies; the agency imposed new, sweeping, and immediate regulatory requirements. However unintentionally, this created an issue for EM physicians, who need to perform on-site, emergent treatments and therefore must be free to employ patient sedation when necessary. (EM physicians are specifically trained for such instances and have immediate access to the life-support equipment necessary for addressing any patient safety issues [breathing usually being the primary concern] during sedation.) This problem was not insignificant and needed to be solved quickly, so I worked with fellow physicians within CMS (and externally as well) to refine the problematic regulations and ensure that patients receiving emergency care would not encounter unnecessary delays in receiving that care.

CMS was in the midst of change when I arrived. Earlier in the year, Congress had passed, and President Obama had signed, the American Recovery and Reinvestment Act of 2009. This historic legislation had many components, but most relevant to my work was the Health Information Technology for Economic and Clinical Health Act, (also known as the HITECH Act.) This legislation poured billions of dollars into the healthcare system's infrastructure to promote greater adoption of EHRs, which were already in use at this time but were by no means universal. HITECH also provided funding for the creation of health information exchanges that would streamline the ways in which various health-record software-systems communicated with each other. As HITECH programs rolled out, I helped bring hospitals, doctors, technology firms, and community collaboratives together to get stronger health-information infrastructures built across Region 5 and ensure that providers adopted these new ways of communicating. I was sure an expansion of EHRs at this scale could be game-changing for the overall healthcare industry, and I was determined to make sure providers understood why this change, including writing and sending prescriptions electronically, was important for advancing healthcare. Additionally, CMS helped create the Meaningful Use program, which offered financial incentives for providers to both use EHRs and offer suggestions for improvement as EHR systems were refined.

I'd long seen the potential EHRs held. I'd been involved with them since their earliest inception—first at Howard, then later at Ingalls Memorial—and having a hand in universalizing EHRs invigorated me. Many times during my residency years at UChicago, retail pharmacies had to call the ED because they couldn't read the handwriting of a physician who'd prescribed an outpatient medication. It also wasn't uncommon for a patient to "bounce back" to the ER (i.e., return soon after being sent home), and when this happened, these patients were sometimes unable to clearly explain their ailments. Back then, to counter issues like these, we kept a pile of the last day's charts in the ER for quick access. Because ER staff knew information mattered, sorting through the pile of charts to find the one needed was normally a minor inconvenience, but sometimes—when paper files had to be retrieved from the medical records room or X-ray/CT-scan films had to be put back up on light boards and reexamined on the spot—the need for EHRs was glaring. Across our nation's healthcare system, the information gap has long contributed to unnecessary duplication of tests, longer patient waiting times, and even patient safety issues. This was (and still is) frustrating for everyone, and now that I was in the hub of the HITECH Act's change, I took every chance I could to conduct outreach and education sessions. I often traveled to sites across Region 5, meeting with small and large groups alike to answer questions, listen to concerns, and advocate for the transformation that full EHR implementation would bring.

Although I enjoyed conducting these sessions, concerns about EHRs from providers abounded. Most trepidations were routine enough that

I had answers at the ready, although occasionally someone threw me a curveball. Once, while I was in one of the Quad Cities (on the Illinois side), during the Q&A session after my main talk, a provider walked to the microphone. This person proclaimed that the mandatory adoption of EHRs was being enacted to increase malpractice cases against physicians because their typically illegible notes in patient records would now be typed out and clear enough for attorneys to use against them. Thankfully, most EHR concerns were far more reasonable, and my physician colleagues brought up many questions that helped CMS better shape the new incentive programs. (In fact, as time went on and many physicians started having patient-radiology-imaging transferred to electronic platforms, I believe they began to see the value in digitizing entire medical records). Today, some of my colleagues still do complain about EHRs, but the work I did at CMS helped improve the quality of care for patients throughout the Midwest. Although it's true that EHR systems aren't perfect (and even now there's still more work to be done to make them even more interoperable), we have certainly come a long way.

In 2010, after President Obama signed into law his landmark Affordable Care Act, which created online exchanges where individuals and families could buy sliding-scale health-insurance plans, I began crisscrossing the Midwest with acting CMS administrator, Dr. Donald Berwick, in part to promote the emerging Shared Savings Program (SSP). SSP aspired to shift healthcare to a more patient-centered approach and transform how CMS paid for value-driven care. (SSP encourages doctors, hospitals, and other healthcare providers to voluntarily join together as an Accountable Care Organization [ACO] to offer coordinated, quality care to Medicare and Medicaid beneficiaries.) This led to ACOs becoming more visible, and soon they became a major framework for patient-centered care-systems where CMS released payments based on the quality and value of provider care, rather than solely by the number of services provided.

As Dr. Berwick and I traveled through Region 5, I learned firsthand how local healthcare really can be. From big cities like Detroit to small towns like Black River Falls (WI), I spoke with patients and community leaders about pervasive challenges and the domino effect that economic roadblocks had on access to care. We discussed how CMS was working to protect access to quality care in rural and underserved areas, and we found resources that could be used to promote the health of their communities. Especially when we visited locales where healthcare was too scarce, it was powerful and enlightening to hear the voices of everyday people as they shared their concerns alongside suggestions for improvement—these meetings taught me that no matter how well-educated and influential any given physician-executive might be, often the best solutions to local problems came from communities themselves. Yet as stark as the healthcare landscape in some neighborhoods could be, we also discovered communities where significant innovation was taking place, where health-system leaders, social organizations, physicians, patient groups, and employers had come together to improve health for everyone. (These bright bastions would soon become early adopters and champions of new CMS programs, programs that were, in part, inspired by their work.)

Our work was wide-reaching, and Dr. Berwick and I engaged with all six states falling under my jurisdiction. With Region 5 being so vast but relatively unpopulated, we sometimes had to stay in crummy hotels or fly from town to town in small planes not much bigger than crop dusters to meet with coalitions of patients, community leaders, and others. Dr. Berwick, building on his vast network from his prior executive role with Boston's Institute for Healthcare Improvement, used the insights we gleaned to create programs like the 2011 Partnership for Patients Campaign, a program that would go on to reduce preventable hospital-acquired conditions by almost nine percent in its first three years alone.[17]

Of the many things I learned from my time at CMS, the most deplorable was my first-time exposure to the underbelly of our healthcare system and the large-scale fraud being committed daily. Because Medicare and Medicaid are government agencies, less-than-scrupulous healthcare providers and businesses sometimes view overcharging or stealing from CMS as a victimless crime—which couldn't be further from the truth, as every fraudulently billed dollar is money that cannot be put toward providing care or improving the health of our nation's most vulnerable. As difficult as it was to believe, I found plenty of evidence pointing to physicians who billed CMS—and who were then paid by CMS—for procedures they never performed. In some cases, when I followed the paper trail, I found fraudulent claims for services occurring in multiple states at the same time. In other cases, durable medical equipment providers would send senior citizens medical equipment that they didn't request or need, and CMS would pay for this equipment as well as associated provider's fees. Some scams duping seniors ran so deep that providers would target elderly patients with advertisements proclaiming, "Direct pay by Medicare," where the corrupt

---

17 Centers for Medicare & Medicaid Services: <https://bit.ly/39wVJBF>

provider would bill CMS directly, sidestepping physicians altogether. Mistaking these adverts for healthcare advice, seniors—for the cost of their co-pay—would buy useless-for-their-needs equipment, with CMS picking up the lion's share of the tab.

Sometimes scams would break the rules with orchestrated tactics designed to save a provider money through illegal practices. One such example is providers who disregard the Emergency Medical Treatment and Active Labor Act (EMTALA), which was passed by Congress in 1986 to ensure that everyone seeking treatment in an ER is evaluated and stabilized on-site, including mothers in active labor. This law should have ended a practice called patient dumping, where those who could not pay for services, or were perceived as not being able to pay, would be denied emergency care, inadequately treated, and/or sent to another hospital for indigent care. Even though my time at CMS came more than two decades after EMTALA was enacted, we often received complaints about hospitals that were not following the rules. As one doctor in a small group of EM physicians within CMS, I was identified as an internal expert on EMTALA violations, and I partnered with the US Health and Human Service's Office of the Inspector General to further reduce patient dumping across multiple regions. In this partnership, I was able to collaborate with my colleagues to close these gaps and reeducate providers and contractors about their obligations under those laws and regulations most applicable to them.

Schemes like these and many other well-documented rackets have long created significant headaches for CMS—and for private insurers as well. It's a shame, because most healthcare providers follow the rules and do their jobs well. From phlebotomists performing routine blood tests to doctors in the ER taking extraordinary measures for critical patients, most healthcare providers want to use CMS's funding to provide and improve care, not line their own pockets. Even still, my colleagues and I reviewed hundreds of case files from hospital investigations, and unfortunately we found many illegal behaviors that put the health and safety of patients behind the financial interests and convenience of healthcare providers. Moreover, in this work, I found significant weaknesses in CMS' oversight processes, weaknesses that made it that much easier to cheat the system and all too often gave repeat violators a pass due to some technicality.

Perhaps even worse than fraud schemes were the cases of neglect and even outright abuse that we uncovered at nursing homes. Whether this abuse resulted from staffing shortages, incompetent care, injuries from falls, avoidable pressure sores, or a failure to act swiftly and appropriately when a patient's condition declined, complaints crossed my desk far too often. Ensuing CMS investigations would often find that any single initial complaint was only the tip of the iceberg—often we found multiple violations of all sorts. We even had to investigate allegations of sexual abuse, as it wasn't uncommon for nursing home facilities to, unbeknownst to residents and their families, house sex offenders. CMS' greatest tools for demanding change were levying these facilities with fines and threatening to withdraw their participation in Medicare; we would also often require failing facilities to submit corrective-action plans, ask the state to perform repeated or surprise inspections, and (if necessary) ask the Federal government to conduct overnight inspections. However, our work at the Federal level was only part of the remedy, as regulatory oversight at the state level was critical in protecting the ailing and elderly.

My Federal service was truly a unique experience, and I remain grateful to have served my country in this way. I enjoyed the extraordinary people with whom I worked, and I learned a tremendous amount about healthcare delivery systems and ways to improve the health of our nation. I might have stayed longer at CMS, but in 2012, opportunity came knocking at my door when I was approached by an association seeking to expand its safety- and quality-improvement efforts across its two-hundred member institutions. The chance was simply too good to pass up.

~

In 2012, the Illinois Hospital Association (IHA) was looking to hire its first physician-executive, and after I had some discussions with an executive search firm, several of my close advisors felt the position would be a strong fit for me. Moving into the role of executive director of the (soon to be renamed) IHA Quality Care Institute included managing an existing team, which was an important addition to my executive toolkit. I reported directly to CEO, Maryjane Wurth, and my job included presenting detailed reports to the board of directors, a twenty-eight-seat panel comprised of hospital- and health-system CEOs from across the state.

Building on my work at CMS, and calling on my understanding of the local nature of healthcare, I continued visiting hospitals in every nook and corner of Illinois. From visiting towns large and small, I began to better understand the hows and whys behind the successes of those hospitals that were able to sustain and grow vibrant healthcare programs. At the same time, I kept my eyes peeled for, and my mind open to, innovative ways of supporting better access and quality of care in communities where patients and hospitals alike struggled to make ends meet.

I traveled frequently, and there were plenty of occasions for me to share the insights I'd learned with those beyond the IHA. I often engaged the state government—including the Illinois Department of Public Health and the Illinois Department of Health and Family Services—and brought Illinoisans' healthcare concerns to those empowered to enact change and offer relief. As a registered state lobbyist, I made frequent trips to Springfield to meet with legislators, much as I had done annually as a member of the ACEP. (Because my position with CMS was Federal, I had resigned from many of my ACEP committees in 2009 to avoid conflicts of interest.) It was a privilege to lobby on the behalf of the IHA, and I believe my lobbying had a direct, meaningful influence on the state government's healthcare policies.

One of my more memorable testimonies to a state legislative committee involved addressing the issues of trauma center deserts and, more specifically, the need for an adult trauma center on the Southside of Chicago. While the city is well known for having many outstanding hospitals, it's also riddled with poverty and violent crime, especially on the Southside. Trauma centers were in reasonable proximity to most other areas of Chicago, yet the neighborhood where the need was extraordinary was located in a trauma desert. This lack of access to care took a deep toll: the distance between the site of an injury and a trauma center translates into transit time, and long transit times lead to delays in care, which can be fatal. In trauma care, we often talk about the "golden hour," a term that refers to the critical nature of the first hour after an injury; high-quality golden-hour care in trauma centers (as opposed to non-trauma centers in ERs and rural hospitals) undoubtedly saves lives. In particular, for those who are victims of gun violence, if their injury occurs more than five miles from a trauma center, the transit-care-delay increases risk of death by twenty-one percent.[18]

Although the state had set up the nation's first trauma system in 1971, hospital participation in the system was voluntary, and financing a trauma center was always the elephant in the room. This led to trauma deserts in many places, including the Southside. Community leaders and elected officials were pushing for a solution, and I was with them all the way. The hearing at which I spoke was one of many on the issue, and I used my time to call the legislator's attention to some of the barriers that needed to be eliminated before the Southside's trauma desert could be cured.

The biggest barrier by far was cost. From a business standpoint, opening an adult, Level I trauma center (i.e. a center that's prepared for the widest possible range of injuries) on the Southside would be a risky investment. A primary requirement for a Level I trauma center is having a full array of specialists on call around the clock, which is expensive in terms of physician compensation and liability insurance costs. As data from other Chicago hospitals showed, many Southsiders in need of trauma care often lived in the poorest pockets and were either uninsured or underinsured; this, in conjunction with the EM-TALA laws, meant any Southside trauma center would surely operate at a perpetual loss. (In fact, this is why the Southside's trauma centers all closed in the 1980s.[19]) Unless the legislators could locate funding—and a lot of it—for the new center, it would become a money pit.

---

18   ABC News 7, Chicago: <https://abc7.ws/3s6HeuF>
19   WBEZ Chicago: <https://bit.ly/38GgUAW>

However, there was a lot of public support for a new Southside trauma center. At the community level, Southsiders, especially those in the most underprivileged areas, felt that the trauma-center safety-net had long failed them, just as ongoing gun violence, under-funded (and thus underperforming) schools, underinvestment in the community, and under-addressed narcotics plagues had failed them. They knew gunshot victims, often Black men, were dying not from the bullet itself, but from high transit times to trauma centers. They felt the time was rife for change, and I did too.

One result of this hearing was the commissioning of a trauma center feasibility study, which was to be led by my colleague Dr. Lamar Hasbrouck, then-director of the Illinois Department of Public Health. While I knew the Southside trauma desert couldn't be solved by one single hearing, when I left the Bilandic Building that day, it was clear that this fight would endure. The right people were now engaged with the issue and the discussions would move forward. Ultimately, UChicago Medicine at Hyde Park, in the heart of the Southside, opened a Level I adult trauma center in 2018. The center has been a success and a benison to those needing trauma care. In some Southside zipcodes, transport times to a trauma center have been reduced by up to nine minutes.[20]

Aside from liaising with the legislature, my primary task during my first year at IHA was to press our member hospitals into prioritizing improved patient safety and care quality. Under my leadership, the IHA Quality Care Institute was renamed the Institute for Innovations and

20 Block Club Chicago: <https://bit.ly/3KABHmH>

Care and Quality, marking the start of several major initiatives. One of these initiatives, the Preventing Re-admissions Through Effective Partnerships program (PREP) aligned with CMS's longstanding priority of reducing re-admissions for its beneficiaries, and I was glad to bring my experience in this area to IHA. (A re-admission is when a recently discharged patient returns to the hospital and is again admitted for care.) However, unlike the CMS program, which focused on readmission of Medicare and Medicaid recipients for *any* reason within thirty days of hospital discharge, PREP addressed preventable re-admissions in the private-insurance space, (i.e., the non-Medicare/Medicaid population). PREP had been funded by Blue Cross and Blue Shield of Illinois one year before I'd arrived at the IHA, and among other things, it had initiated new data-analysis reports for member hospitals; this helped individual hospitals better evaluate their past performance, predict future re-admissions, and develop custom interventions that would keep patients from being re-admitted. From my experience at CMS, I knew how important it was to have timely and actionable data, and with these new reports IHA was able to have more timely conversations with its member hospitals about their performance, which was refreshing. We learned that there were broad opportunities to help our member hospitals with re-education on best discharge procedures, and to re-imagine the relationships they had with post-acute-care facilities.

As another bridge back to my CMS service, I was the executive sponsor for our statewide Partnership for Patients (PFP) program. This was a program that CMS had started during my tenure, but since it was underwritten by a branch of the American Hospital Association, the program itself wasn't tied to a physical CMS location. Over one hundred state hospitals took part in PFP, and through collaborative work with hospital staffs and implementing new education programs, we helped improve care across ten national patient harm [prevention] priorities. Between 2012 and 2014, our efforts prevented an estimated 16,000 instances of patient harm and saved more than $161 million in healthcare costs. This was a win all around, but for me, personally, I was imbued with a great sense of satisfaction and fulfillment; I helped improve healthcare at scale, which is why I'd pursued a healthcare leadership position in the first place.

While it was rewarding to see large-scale improvements in action, I was well aware of, and deeply knowledgeable about, inequity in health status and healthcare delivery in pockets of Illinois. With so much state and regional travel as an executive under my belt, and because of my years of experience in the ER, in 2013, I was invited to the White House Achieving eHealth Equity Summit. Here I joined a select group of leaders across government, healthcare, the technology sector, and various experts on health disparities; our charge was to make certain that technology would serve as an asset in terms of closing disparities, and to ensure that the specific technologies used would, in no way, widen disparities.

We gathered for our daylong meeting in the White House's Eisenhower Executive Office Building, and our energy was high. With every seat around the large table taken and many chairs along the room's perimeter occupied, the importance of our work at the summit became even clearer. We spent the day discussing and contemplating the digital landscape that was increasingly touching every aspect of our lives, both inside and outside of medicine. The summit was pivotal for me because it brought into plain sight the importance of addressing health-equity issues with great intention and assiduousness. The colloquialism, "A rising tide lifts all boats," isn't necessarily true, especially if your boat is anchored to the seabed by a short chain that can't be removed without help, much as those facing healthcare disparities—hospital deserts, lack of insurance, low-quality care, (etc.,)—wouldn't be able to lift themselves up without large-scale action from the government.

I was honored to be invited to the White House as a part of this work. The summit once again proved to me the power of creating calls to action, and more personally, it challenged me to consider the barriers I had overcome to reach my career aspirations. After the meeting adjourned, as I walked down the steps of the Eisenhower building, I reflected upon my journey as a physician-leader: as a teenager, I had questioned whether I could become a physician, and as an early resident, I had wondered if I could truly expand into executive health-leadership, where I could influence systems of care. Drawing inspiration from my ancestors, I pursued my dreams, and despite having many doors remain closed when I'd knocked, I was blessed to achieve my dual goal of becoming a physician and an executive. At the same time, however, the opportunities afforded to me by my medical degree and my education were not just for me—they were for the next generation as well. Likewise, the lessons I learned from my patients were not just to benefit my medical skills and knowledge. The insights that I learned at community meetings were not just to make me sharper for the next meeting. My invitation to the White House was not just about ehealth equity. Just like many of the professors I admired at Howard, I was creating a legacy in healthcare—a legacy bigger than me, that would outlast me, that would improve healthcare for millions of Americans for many years to come.

I stayed with IHA until I was recruited to a vice president position at the Health Care Service Corporation (HCSC) in 2014. I founded a new department that was focused on advancing clinical quality and health-plan accreditation at the enterprise level. My team's work was having a measurable, appreciable impact across the five states where HCSC operated as Blue Cross and Blue Shield. In 2018, I moved into a market-facing role at HCSC as vice president and chief medical officer of Blue Cross and Blue Shield of Illinois. Especially because I knew the Illinois healthcare landscape so well, I embraced this chance to lead even as challenges—both emerging and persistent—presented themselves regularly. Yet the biggest of these challenges began in 2019 and is still ongoing at the time of this writing: the COVID-19 pandemic.

In late 2019, a new and highly infectious virus, the SARS-CoV-2 coronavirus, emerged in China and began spreading around the world with alarming alacrity. The resulting and too-often-fatal respiratory illness was deemed COVID-19, and—although the World Health Organization and governments around the world immediately began working to contain it—by late January of 2020, the first cases had hit the US. By March of that year, cases in the US (and around the globe) were doubling and tripling like wildfire. With so little known about the virus and essentially no effective treatments yet created for severe cases, US states began issuing stay-at-home orders for residents, and non-essential services (including entire school systems) were shut down.[21]

The pandemic brought unprecedented challenges to healthcare delivery systems as we struggled to understand the virus, save the lives of patients, and protect the health of frontline workers. During the height

---

21 Centers for Disease Control: <https://bit.ly/3FkE24h>

of the first year of the pandemic, as many regular hospital services were shut down to create surge capacity for COVID-19 victims, patients had few places to seek non-emergency care, while others deferred care from reasonable fears of being exposed to COVID-19 at a healthcare facility. As a healthcare leader I, along with many colleagues and partners, began rapidly expanding access to telehealth services to help meet the need for non-emergency care. (Health care providers were also able to work more easily across state lines due to licensing relaxations.) We worked to adjust our systems to accommodate the temporary waiver of insurance co-pays as mandated under various public-health-emergency orders; these were put in place so that the millions who were losing income from the shutdowns could better afford routine care. These mandated waivers included access to virtual mental health services. While the pre-pandemic demand for mental healthcare was greater than the supply in many locations, the overarching impact of lockdowns and isolation, the loss of family and friends to the virus, and the perpetual fear and anxiety about illness caused many Americans to seek mental health care for the first time in their lives. Both during and after the lockdowns, better access to mental healthcare using telehealth has been among the very, very few silver linings to emerge from the pandemic.

At a time when so much of the nation was focused on avoiding the virus and keeping themselves healthy, I found myself constantly filling the information and trust gap for the public. I began providing necessary education to local, regional, and national audiences, and at every opportunity, I spoke on infection prevention steps such as social/physical distancing, wearing masks and other facial coverings properly, and frequent handwashing. In early 2021, when the first emergency-use COVID-19 vaccines became available to the general public, I expanded this advocacy to include the safety, efficacy, and importance of these inoculations. With well over American lives lost to the pandemic,[22] I'm grateful to have influenced or even saved many lives through my many presentations, media appearances, and spearheaded discussions—and this has perhaps been the greatest honor of my career. To date, over seventy percent of Illinois' eligible population have received at least one dose of a vaccine,[23] and as we move into new battles with this virus, I'll continue my work until a permanent solution is found. In fact, tonight (January 5th, 2022), as the surge of this fifth wave rages, I am headed to the frontlines in the ER to fight COVID-19 and help save lives.

---

22 As of the last data available at the time of this writing. Centers for Disease Control: <https://bit.ly/3KCJ2Sy>

23 As of the last data available at the time of this writing. Illinois: <https://bit.ly/3OQ8Eib>

DEREK ROBINSON: FATHER, HUSBAND, BROTHER, DOCTOR, ADVOCATE

CHAPTER 15

Becoming a Father

As a teenager and a young adult, I was not a big fan of little kids. While I always dreamed of being a father, however paradoxically, diapers, runny noses, meltdowns, sleepless nights, and all that stuff were not at the top of my list of things to do. Later, while in medical school, after developing just a small understanding of the many things that can go wrong during pregnancy, I realized how blessed we are to have healthy children in our lives. But perhaps my biggest pro-child shift came just after Shawn and I got engaged. Both of us had deferred many things in our lives, including having kids, to become physicians. As busy and focused as we were, we hoped and prayed that we would someday become loving parents fully engaged with our children's upbringing.

In 2011, on a hot Saturday morning just outside of Atlanta, during a time in my career when I worked clinically some weekends in the area, I was on shift as one of two attending physicians in a busy emergency department. The day was proving to be fast-paced, with the usual types of cases—chest pain, abdominal pain, lacerations, strokes—coming in at a good clip. Our team was working smoothly that day, but the demand kept coming. By the middle of my shift, I was managing about sixteen patients (at various stages of their workups) and overseeing a physician's assistant who was caring for eight patients. None of the craziness was getting to me, though, because I was looking forward to my upcoming month-long vacation, which would begin as soon as I was back in Chicago. And this would be no ordinary vacation either, as I was about to embark on the greatest journey of my life: Fatherhood.

In the ED that day, as usual, both my personal and work smartphones, each of which was serviced by a different mobile carrier, were clipped to the waistband of my scrubs. (For tax and other reasons, in the earlier years of the twenty-first century, it wasn't unusual for executives in almost any field to carry two phones.) Having two different mobile service providers was especially beneficial for me: emergency departments are notoriously windowless, and the hospitals that house them are often huge—a given carrier's service can be spotty in some areas even when another carrier is functioning fairly well. As I was walking down the hall, my personal phone rang a few times but stopped abruptly. I glanced at the screen and saw that I didn't have service, so I continued toward my patient's room. While at his bedside, my wife was calling my work phone, which was unusual. I excused myself and stepped into the hall.

Shawn, giggling with delight, was initially coy about why she was calling; she had a challenge for me to maneuver through but conveyed all the confidence in the world that I could do it. Although she had just arrived home after her overnight shift in the neonatal intensive care unit, her water had broken, and our first child was on his way. This was exciting and joyful news, except that I was in Atlanta while she was in Chicago—I never imagined that we would be so far apart when this blessed moment was upon us. I mentally jumped for joy but hit my head on the ceiling of fear; I was still at work, in a dynamic clinical environment, where the team and my patients needed me. As I had done many times before in stressful moments, I kept my emotions in check as Shawn and I talked. We ended the call by outlining her game plan: she would grab a few things from our home, then head straight to the delivery ward at her hospital, where her co-workers would care for her during her labor. I, on the other hand, needed to figure out how to get back to Chicago, a feat that would include successfully navigating many factors that were simply beyond my control.

The moment we hung up, my thoughts started racing. How could Shawn be in labor? We'd visited her obstetrician on Thursday, and everything was on track—our child's due date remained almost one month away. We'd planned pretty well for our son's arrival, too. I'd boarded my flight to Atlanta on Friday night for my last two shifts before vacation; I had planned to fly home Sunday evening. Shawn's last two shifts had been scheduled for Friday night and Saturday night, with her maternity leave beginning on Sunday. Yet, despite all our prep, as I was quickly learning, our plans had nothing to do with reality: the next twelve hours would be about how flexible we could be.

Especially when Shawn's pregnancy had progressed to its later stages, the other physicians in her group were very accommodating. They well knew that babies arrive on their own schedules, and so they had made plans to cover Shawn in case she went into labor earlier than expected. Yet as for me, I was faced with a multi-faceted dilemma. I needed to ensure that my patients were cared for and safe, avoid placing any unnecessary stress on the only other attending in the ED, convince another EM doctor to cover for me, and fly home in time to celebrate the birth of our first child. I had a lot to do and very little time to do it, and much of that first hour after Shawn's call remains a blur. I do, however, remember walking over to the other attending on shift as she typed at her computer to explain why I had to leave. I opened with, "I have good news and bad news." I don't recall her really looking up from the screen, but I did sense that her stress level was rising as she thought about the possibility of having to run the entire department alone.

Trying not to think of the many potential obstacles between me and Chicago, I sent out an urgent email to our group of EM physicians. Dr. Boykin Robinson, who lived nearby, came in to cover for me, and I am forever grateful to him. As I told my patients they would be transferred into my colleague's care, each one was understanding about my need to leave. In fact, one patient, an elderly woman, told me flat out, "Baby, you need to get home to see about your wife. I'll be just fine, don't worry about me." With my professional responsibilities properly addressed, I called Delta Air Lines to change my ticket to the next available flight to Chicago. I don't know how stressed I must've sounded on the phone, but the representative kindly accommodated my request and confirmed my new seat number.

Still in my scrubs, I hopped in my rental car and made a beeline for my friend's home where I was staying to grab my still-partially-unpacked bag; I stuffed everything back in the small suitcase and was out the door in two minutes. Back in the car, I prayed that the Atlanta traffic wouldn't jam up as it so often did. My prayer was answered, and the traffic flow to the airport's grounds was decent. When I exited the highway at Camp Creek Parkway, I faced my last bit of driving—a seemingly unnecessary two-and-a-half-mile stretch to the airport's car rental center. After parking the car in the drop off-lane and then sprinting up the escalators to the shuttle train level, I grabbed a seat on a departing train to the Hartsfield-Jackson Atlanta International Airport, where I was the first person off, down the stairs, across the walkway, and into the terminal. At this point, there were only twenty-five minutes before my flight; time was ticking away, yet I still needed to get through airport security. That day, I was in luck as the expedited security lane was open; my frequent-flyer status allowed me to get through in only a few minutes with my carry-on luggage. By now I was truly nervous about the possibility of missing my son's birth, but I knew from my medical training that a mother's labor for the first child is usually prolonged—I was banking on it to buy me some time. With precious minutes slipping away, I hopped onto the terminal shuttle train and was at my gate inside of a few moments. My plane was in sight at last, and once aboard, I managed to settle into my seat just before takeoff.

The flight was two excruciating hours long, although a quick video call with Shawn assured me all was well on her end. On my phone's screen, I could see her calm, smiling face, and I noted that an IV bag of Pitocin was hanging at her bedside, which she said was set to a low drip. (With fewer barriers between me and Chicago, her doctor had felt comfortable using a low dose of Pitocin to begin advancing her labor.) Also comforting was knowing that my mother-in-law, who lived four hours away in Detroit, had dropped everything to be with her daughter while she labored. I knew we were in the home stretch now, and every ounce of me wished I were already at my wife's side. Soon (but not soon enough for my liking) I landed at Chicago's Midway airport around 7:00 p.m.—on time and with no weather delays—and called Shawn as I disembarked. She never said, "Derek, you better make it here in time," but I knew that was what she was thinking, even as she herself assured me that I had time to make it to the hospital. A grateful-ness swept through me: the drive from the airport to the hospital was only twenty minutes long—I would be at my wife's side for the birth of our first child.

A few hours after I arrived, our son Grant was born. He was pre-cious, and along with my elation, I felt an immediate responsibility for his well-being. The moment he came into this world, I wanted to raise him in the air like Rafiki did to Simba in the *Lion King*, but Grant was still slippery from the birthing fluids, so I settled for cutting his umbil-ical cord. Our son was almost a month ahead of our best planning, but really, he was right on time—and he was as healthy as could be. That night, Grant slept in the bassinet in Shawn's hospital room as I curled up in a reclining chair at her bedside. Just after dawn broke, with the sun rising over Lake Michigan and shining in through the window, I eased over in my chair and picked Grant up. There in the dawn light came one of the most sacred moments of my life as I snuggled my son in my arms, watching his toothless yawns and graceful sleep. A stillness enveloped us; the hospital faded away. It was a quiet moment to enjoy and savor this cherished life.

Once home, we were fortunate enough to have my mother-in-law with us for the first few days. Her visit was followed by a visit from my mom, who came up from Louisiana to meet her new grandson. After about a week at home with my family, I returned to work and Shawn continued her twelve weeks of maternity leave. Our mothers both had left by this time, and although we had no family locally to lend a help-ing hand, we managed to make things work. I marveled at my son's ap-petite: every few hours, night and day alike, he would awake and want to be fed. The sleeplessness was hard on Shawn and me both, and—as much as I adored him—some nights I thought Grant was destined to be an only child unless things got easier very soon. Yet "soon" took a while to come, as it was a good seven months before Shawn and I figured out how to get Grant to sleep through the night: at bedtime, if given expressed, bottled breast milk (rather than feeding at the breast) he would drink a few extra ounces. An extra-full stomach was the key to a deep and lasting sleep for our son—and for us—and finally I had hope that he might not be an only child.

As two first-time parents with demanding careers and irregular schedules, when it came time for Shawn to return to her duties at the hospital, we had to juggle our schedules. As a physician-executive rather than a full-time clinician, I had a little more flexibility than Shawn, and I was able to adjust my schedule so I could work from home during the days when she was on shift. With a little practice, I was able to time my feeding and cuddling sessions so that my little guy would be asleep when I had conference calls. My system wasn't perfect of course, and more than once Grant's cries prompted gentle chiding from my colleagues with comments like, "Hey, is there a baby on this call?" A collective chuckle would follow as everyone knew I had an infant at home, and they were all happy for our family.

Adjusting our schedules in the short-term was one thing, but we still had to figure out our permanent childcare arrangements. We knew that choosing a caretaker was the most important decision in front of us: we had to make the right move for our son. We considered the pros and cons of daycare alongside the limitations that mandatory pick-up and drop-off times would impose on our work hours, and we decided that in-home help was our best option. But finding a nanny proved to be among the most painstaking and frustrating processes that I can recall from our early years as parents. For the next three or four weeks, our days were consumed by résumé reading, phone interviews, reference checking and background checks, and in-person interviews. In the end, we were fortunate to be blessed with an excellent nanny who would care for and love our son as if he were her own. To this day, I believe hiring her was the single best decision we made, and the single best blessing we received, as young parents.

Two years after my first son was born, Shawn and I were again expecting a child. Having learned our lesson from Grant's birth, this time we planned our schedules around a possible early delivery—and I made sure I wouldn't be caught out of town again. My mother timed a visit with us during Shawn's final weeks of pregnancy as she had been placed on bed rest by her doctor, who thought she might deliver early. (Other than that, Shawn's pregnancy had been healthy and uncomplicated—a blessing for us all.) Fortunately, Shawn had reached full term by the night her water broke, and thanks to my mother, my wife and I were able to head to the hospital knowing that Grant was cared for. We could now focus our energy on greeting and welcoming our second child.

It was 6:05 a.m. when our baby came into the world that April morning. We had chosen not to find out our baby's gender until birth, and as I stood on Shawn's left side holding her hand, I watched with anticipation and eagerness. The doctor then announced that we had a baby boy! I proudly cut Reid's umbilical cord as he cried vigorously, and a nurse placed him on Shawn's chest for the first time. Later that day, I marveled at Reid's bluish-gray eyes staring quietly back at me, and I wondered if his eye color, once permanent, would be hazel like mine. It wasn't long afterward that Grandma (my mother) arrived with

Grant; both were ecstatic, and Grant, now a big brother, "approved" of the new addition to our family. With Reid being only a few hours old, we took the first photo of all four of us together.

Because the delivery was uncomplicated, and because Shawn and Reid were doing well at the end of the second day, they were discharged and sent home. That night, in our bedroom, I watched as Shawn gave Reid his last feeding of the day, and then, at about 10:00 p.m. I settled our newest miracle into the bassinet at our bedside. With jest in my voice, I asked my wife if she wanted me to take the first shift and feed him when he woke up, knowing full well that she hadn't expressed any milk yet—all feedings for the time being had to come directly from her. She laughed at my joke, and we gazed at our infant son one more time before calling it a night. Since we now knew what to expect, we assumed Reid would awake in a few hours, and we braced ourselves for the impending state of sleep deprivation to come. Five hours later, at 3:00 a.m., we found ourselves peering over the edge of the bassinet perplexed and alarmed: we hadn't once heard a peep from Reid. We checked his respiratory rate and assessed his skin color for signs of lack of oxygen, but thankfully he was breathing easily and was simply still asleep. It wasn't until 5:45 a.m. that he stirred, ready for his first feeding. That morning, my wife looked well-rested, and I was excited for the day ahead because my sleep had been pretty much undisturbed. As the first weeks with our second child flew by, we realized Reid didn't take after his brother: our youngest would sleep through the night and awake early in the morning. Shawn and I were grateful for this benison; if we hadn't had Grant first, we never would've fully appreciated the gift Reid gave us by letting us have steady, full nights' sleeps. Even to this day, Reid is my early riser, and we get up at about the same time, while the other two members of our household will sleep late if given even half a chance.

The next few years with the boys brought us many memorable moments. From their first words and first steps, to Reid's predilection for dumping his food on his head, to Grant's coaching his little brother on how to eat, these years were full of laughs. Both boys were fascinated with going through our kitchen drawers and cabinets and pulling out our colorful Tupperware; if I turned my back for even a second, I would find containers and lids sprawled across the floor. I felt as if I were in a Comedy Central program in the days after I installed cabinet safety locks, first for Grant (in our first home) and later for Reid after we moved. Both boys were similarly perplexed—why wouldn't the cabinets open anymore? —and pulled at them repeatedly until they had to accept defeat.

Diapers were a part of my life for a long time, and it was Grant, at only a few months old, who taught me just how explosive a baby's diaper can be. The timing couldn't have been worse: we were at an outside food festival in the West Loop, where those in the crowd were enjoying their meals and treats. It was a warm summer day, and I was carrying Grant in a gray-and-white baby carrier while we walked around. That's when I heard the not-unusual squirting sounds of my son pooping. What was unusual was when the foul-smelling, orange-tinged poop began leaking from his diaper and seeping down his legs and onto my clothes. I was a mess, he was a mess—we both had to leave, and I bolted out of there as quickly as I could. That day, I learned from experience not to have the bottom of the baby carrier fit so snug in the future.

Among my absolute favorite memories of my early years as a father has its roots in a winter evening when Shawn told me that she'd booked us a hotel for a Jack and Jill Family Ski Weekend. I intuitively knew I was in trouble. I'd never stepped foot on a ski slope, and I was wary of the many stories I'd heard about skiers running into trees and breaking their legs. Nevertheless, my wife was certain that we were going, and since she learned how to ski growing up, she wanted the boys to learn as well—meaning, essentially, that I would be learning to ski at the same time as my sons. Our first trip was to Cascade Mountain in Wisconsin. Grant was just shy of five years old, and we enrolled him in the little kids' class. At the time, Reid was only two years old, and although he was dressed for the slopes in his snowsuit and goggles, he stayed in the resort with our friend Cheryl during our lessons, where he was spoiled silly for the afternoon.

Even the basics of skiing challenged me: How do I put on a ski boot? Do the legs of my ski pants go inside my boot or outside? Walking with Grant to the pro shop with our boots on to select our skis was like walking with a cast on both legs, with me hoping not to fall on top of my son. Once fitted with our skis, getting from the pro shop across a flat stretch to the site of our classes seemed to take an eternity. I couldn't quite get my momentum going, and for an instant the father-son dynamic flipped. Grant had figured out how to shuffle himself forward, so I did what he did. We learned the basics from our respective classes, then managed to ski a few bunny hills together, with the two of us holding hands the whole way down.

Two years later, during another Jack and Jill Ski Weekend, Grant and I had our biggest adventure yet. We were at a ski resort in Galena, IL, which overlooked the frozen Mississippi River. Reid was old enough now for the little kids' class, with the rest of us taking refresher courses. Afterward, Shawn went off with Reid, while Grant and I took a couple of small hills together. Both of us had made progress since our first skiing trip; the only difference between the two of us was that I had fear and Grant did not. He quickly became bored with the small hills and was really ribbing on me to go down a bigger hill with him. I relented when it came time for the last slope of the evening. As we moved towards the top of the hill, the sun was just starting to set, and the run's lights were turning on. The slope's initial decline was gentle, but then, as the ski run turned to the left, it became steep with a clear drop off; I wondered if I'd made a mistake in choosing this run.

As we began at the very top of the hill, Grant, as he often was, was about ten feet in front of me. I called out, asking him to show me his breaking skills, and almost as if it were second nature, he began skiing side-to-side in an S pattern as he'd been taught. When we approached the hill's first and only turn, my little seven-year-old son, whose safety and well-being had been entrusted to me by both a Divine hand and my wife herself, took off down the hill. A novice skier at best, I pursued him; I called after him, reminding him to go side-to-side to control his speed as he navigated the turn. Grant, however, had something different in mind: going straight. Racing after him, I watched in horror as he picked up more and more speed. We approach a ski jump on the left side of the run, and my heart almost stopped at the thought of his catapulting himself into the air and possibly off the nearby precipice. To my relief, Grant avoided the jump, but then he lost his footing and tumbled into the snow. I was finally able to catch up with him. When I was about six feet away from him, I asked him if he was okay, and Grant looked up at me laughing. I got him back on his feet and was afforded a moment or two of relief before he turned around and proceeded to start the process all over again. I went after him, thinking all the while that Shawn was going to kill me if something happened to our eldest son. Grant, meanwhile, was having a blast—no breaking, no snowplowing, no side-to-side *S* pattern—the kid just kept going straight, picking up speed all the while. With my fear still growing, he continued downward until, with about a third of the hill left to go, he finally tumbled again and fell into a snowdrift. I was on my way to him when a gentleman on a snowboard, with a beer in one hand, helped Grant stand up. This is where my son's independent adventure came to an end. With me keeping an even closer eye on him now, we skied to the bottom of the hill together safely.

Reid almost matched his brother in terms of keeping me on my toes. When I think of his early childhood, I often remember one particular Christmas Eve. We were in Shreveport for the holidays, and that morning Reid and I set out to go fishing on the lake behind my dad's house. The morning was so foggy, I could barely see the cypress trees out by the lake. Yet I was determined to make it to the pier because I had decided that today would be Reid's very first fishing trip—after all, he was my early riser, and I knew he'd be excited to go fishing with me despite our starting at dawn. There were certainly no guarantees that we would catch anything that morning, but I wanted to enhance our chances, so while the fog burned off the lake, we made a run to a local bait and tackle shop, where the shelves were lined with everything from snacks to various types of outdoor equipment. My son was initially mostly interested in the snacks, but I knew he was in for a real treat when he saw the live bait on offer, so I steered him toward the large well where the minnows were kept. Too short to see over the ledge, Reid asked me to pick him up so he could see what was in the water. His eyes lit up when he saw hundreds of tiny fish swimming around in the well.

When the salesperson asked how many minnows we wanted, I handed him our bucket and asked for two dozen. Reid immediately wanted to stick his hand in the bucket to grab a minnow, but I reminded him that this was just the beginning of our fishing trip. We then went on to buy one-dozen Canadian nightcrawlers, a type of large worm. As was customary, the clerk emptied our container of worms onto a small tray so we could see that the live bait was, in fact, still alive. With a puzzled look of curiosity, Reid frowned—the worms were as wide as his pinky finger, and the wiggling creatures were apparently not to his liking. On the other hand, though, when we selected a cageful of two-dozen brown crickets, the insects fascinated Reid. He held the wired container up to his face and smiled at the crickets that clung to its side.

On the pier behind my father's house, wearing the yellow-and-blue life jacket that his brother had worn two or three years back, Reid walked down the pier with his cane fishing pole, which was about three times longer than he was tall. Our first task was to get his line in the water, but only after he made his choice of bait. Attracted by their movement and chirping, Reid went for the crickets. This led to what I now call the "cricket comedy." Not knowing how to handle the insects, Reid scrambled along behind an escaped cricket, his eyes and hands darting, as the insect jumped away time after time. When he tried another cricket, the same thing happened—jump, jump, jump, with Reid following behind, almost as if in a cartoon. It was pure fun watching him go after cricket after cricket after cricket. Laughing, I let him pursue the bugs, although I watched him carefully to ensure that he didn't become so distracted as to fall straight into the lake.

Finally, I grabbed a minnow, put it on Reid's hook, and at last began the fishing part of our fishing trip. I then baited several more fishing poles and put them in a few strategic locations to increase his chances of catching a fish on his first-ever fishing trip. Meanwhile, Reid was fully engaged with the minnow on his hook—up and down, around in circles, in and out of the water, his baitfish was on a ride as he impatiently waited for a bite. Probably thanks to the extra enthusiasm with his bait, we didn't have a bite on the line for a long while. Bored with the minnow in the water, Reid then turned to splashing around in the minnow bucket. It was still a good while before the bobber on his line quivered and his cane pole bent in an arc—Reid had his first bite! Filled with excitement, I came up behind him, quickly showing him the signs of having a fish on his hook. I placed the pole in his hands and helped him lift the fish; he felt the weight and vibrations of the fish, which got him really excited. We pulled the line up and saw a big, thrashing catfish! The creature was about sixteen inches long and it was heavy. Reid's voice filled with gleeful enthusiasm, "I've got a fish! I've got a fish!" We continued hauling in his catch together but, unfortunately, his line snapped suddenly and broke off. My son's joy-filled face was overtaken with disappointment, and an inconsolable frown appeared. He looked into the water for the catfish again and again, but the creature didn't swim back. A few minutes passed and then, with all of the patience of a five-year-old, Reid was done with fishing and ready to go eat breakfast.

It's no fun fishing with a young child who doesn't want to be at your side, so I quickly changed the bait on two of our other poles, then checked to make sure they were well-secured to the pier. I hadn't given up on winning my son over to fishing, although I knew it would require some patience. We went on with our morning, catching up with Grant, my dad, and the rest of our family. In the afternoon, both my boys wanted to go down to the pier, and I joined them to check on our poles. As we approached them, it was clear we had a fish on one of the lines. Reid, about as excited as he could be, wanted to make sure that we didn't lose this fish; my advice on how to save the catch was quickly rebuffed by both Reid and Grant as they had a plan. With his brother at his side, Reid carefully lifted the fish out of the water, landing it on the wooden pier; he jumped and laughed as the large white perch flopped around. After a moment, I grabbed the fish by its lower lip and removed the hook from its mouth. Incredibly proud of my son, I asked Reid what he wanted to do with his first catch. He hesitantly reached out to touch the fish's slimy scales, then recoiled as if the perch had jumped with his touch. Satisfied that he caught a fish, Reid wanted to let it go, so I released it back into the water.

Thinking back to my life before kids, it was certainly a good one. My focus was on my career, my large and sprawling family, my broader community, and my own needs. Those needs included companionship, which led to my marrying Shawn, who is a wonderful wife, mother, and partner. So distant now are the memories of our spontaneous date nights, quick trips out of town, or heart-stopping adventures like our safari in South Africa where we found ourselves twenty yards from a pride of sleeping lions. Yet neither freedom nor fun trump the many rewards and joys of fatherhood itself. My transition to being a dad brought me a sense of conservatism and risk-aversion, along with persistent concern about the long-term consequences of the decisions Shawn and I make for our boys. Innocent, vulnerable, and malleable, my sons introduced me to a new world of possibilities, opportunities, and responsibilities. My love for them elevated my patience; teaching them from their mistakes taught me how to truly forgive and forget, and my hopes for them taught me the importance of investing my time in them, instilling morals and values in them, and giving them a solid foundation upon which they can build their individual senses of confidence as they develop their interests.

I've had many people tell me that parenting over the years becomes a blur, and now, with Grant in his tween years and Reid soon to follow, I understand why. Being a father is a dynamic, twenty-four seven experience; keeping up with it all is sometimes like living in a whirl. As the boys have grown older, their cuteness has given way to individual personalities—Grant is curious and confident, while Reid is energetic and thoughtful. They make me proud in so many ways, but perhaps I am most proud of their inseparable bond as brothers. Woven into the fabric of their brotherhood is a healthy sense of sibling rivalry, a commitment to family, and an insatiable desire to compete athletically. In love, Shawn, the boys, and I look forward to continuing to grow spiritually, capturing key moments together, learning life lessons, reaffirming our trust in each other and in humanity itself, and putting the needs of others before our own.

CHAPTER 16

When Being a Doctor Wasn't Enough

In late December 1992, I went to see my paternal grandparents as I usually did around Christmastime. Like always, when I arrived Granddad was sitting on the porch in his blue overalls, corduroy flannel shirt, and hat, with his legs crossed and his dogs at his side. Inside, my grandmother was cooking in the long, narrow kitchen at the back of the house. The aroma of her food drew me to the stove, where I was delighted to find collard greens, hot-water corn bread, and lightly fried pork chops being cooked up. I was hungry, so I was relieved to find that my grandmother wasn't stewing squirrel. While I'd always enjoyed my hunting trips with my father, Grandad, and occasionally my brother, I was never a fan of eating the fox squirrels we caught.

While the three of us were catching up, someone knocked on the front door. A few moments later, my grandfather introduced me to my second-oldest sister Linda. She and her husband Chris were visiting from their home in Australia for the holidays. They were expecting their first child, and Linda was visibly pregnant with my niece Laia. Meeting my sister was joyful and brought me a strange sense of relief— my father had never brought us together as a family, but now that I was old enough, I could reach out to my siblings and begin filling in the gaps between us. (Until this point, I'd only met my brother a handful of times, usually on fishing trips.) When I met Linda, some long-dormant part of me opened to the possibility of becoming a part of my father's family.

Before the holidays were over, Linda—who had limited time on her visit and wanted to make every single day count—invited me to dinner so I could meet my two other sisters, Sharon and Deborah. Not knowing exactly what to expect, I was a bit nervous and emotionally guarded going into the meal—I knew my sisters already had a younger brother, and I wasn't too sure they wanted another one. With the dinner being for me and "the girls" only, I was on my own for the night, since neither my dad nor my brother would be joining us. My sisters and I gathered at a Piccadilly in a local mall, and from the very moment we sat down, it was obvious the three were a remarkably close group. From there, the evening was authentically uncomfortable. I was a high-school student and ten years younger than the youngest of the three, so they all handled me with kid gloves. This first meeting should've been joyous, but the situation was more complicated than that: my presence, at a minimum, made real the pain of my dad's decisions. In fact, the evening was a bit too much for my oldest sister Deborah, especially given my resemblance to our father, and she left the restaurant early with her young son—my nephew Anthony—in tow. I initially didn't comprehend her reaction to meeting me, but after talking with Linda later, I was better able to understand why she'd been so overwhelmed: the situation was new to us all; we all needed to meet each other where we were emotionally; and only then could we grow together from there. We had to decide the type and the quality of our relationship as siblings, and our building that relationship would take openness and effort on all our parts.

With time, Deborah, Linda, Sharon, and I built a shared trust, allowing us to grow closer. I had a young nephew to get to know and an infant niece growing up on the other side of the world in Sydney. We had much to share with each other, and my sisters and I stayed connected throughout my undergraduate years. Since Sharon and Deborah shared an apartment, I was able to visit with them in one shot when I was home from college, while Linda and I regularly exchanged hand-written letters between New Orleans and Sydney. When I moved to Washington DC for medical school, and later after I relocated to Chicago to begin my post-MD career, my sisters and I saw each other on holidays and at special family events, and we made time for regular letters, phone calls, and emails. Even better, the relationships I formed with my sisters opened an entirely new aspect of life for me: being an uncle. Over the years, my nephew Anthony grew into a standout football player, ultimately playing as center on his college's championship team. Down under, my niece Laia became a national figure skating champion who went on to compete internationally. One year, when she was competing in the Bavarian Alps, Shawn and I went to Germany to show support. Later, when Laia skated in the 2010 Winter Olympics in Vancouver, we were absolutely thrilled when the US television stations cut to her during her performance. Being an involved uncle with my sisters' children led to my connecting with my brother's daughter, Melanie. She too was an athlete; in high school, she competed in track-and-field events at the state-championship level. I'm proud to be an uncle to all of them. Through the years, we've had a lot to celebrate as a family.

During my medical school years, storm clouds began creeping into our lives. Now in her late thirties, Deborah developed weight-related, type 2 diabetes. In the blink of an eye, I went from being her sweet younger brother to her (undoubtedly annoying) health coach. I hated seeing my normally upbeat and cheerful sister struggling with health challenges, and as a medical student, I wanted to help all I could— even when she didn't necessarily want that help. Sometimes Deborah was open to my advice, but often she distanced herself from me and my seemingly-never-ending recommendations. I pushed her as far as I dared until she firmly reminded me that I wasn't a doctor quite yet. Her defensiveness stung a little, although her words, however unwittingly, taught me an important lesson about respecting others' limits and sharing my growing medical knowledge judiciously. Essentially, Deborah didn't sign up for a family health coach, and I had to respect her boundaries while also stepping up when she asked for my help.

By the time I finished medical school, Deborah's diabetes was leading to other health issues, including heart and kidney disease. During my years as a resident, my sister's trips to the emergency room became increasingly common, as did her hospitalizations. To avoid worrying us, sometimes she would sneak off for treatment without telling anyone. In fact, her code phrase to me when she was hospitalized was, "I'm on vacation, in the hotel," and that's how I knew she really wasn't okay. I often felt frustrated that I couldn't do more: as a resident of Chicago, I was over eight hundred miles away from Shreveport, and I couldn't watch her mannerisms or determine if her facial expressions matched the brightness in her voice, nor could I monitor how winded she got when doing even simple tasks. This put me in a difficult, awkward position because Deborah was very good at concealing her symptoms when we spoke on the phone—even when she wasn't feeling at all well, she rarely revealed the true depth of her struggle, pain, and fear. Like my mom, Deborah was a single parent who devoted herself to her son's wellbeing, and I suspect she spent more time worrying about Anthony than thinking of her own illness. In some ways, I admired her for that, but I often had to resort to asking Sharon and their mom subtle medical questions about Deborah's state to get a real handle on her health status.

In the summer of 2014, due to her worsening heart function, Deborah's local specialist referred her to a New Orleans medical center for a cardiology evaluation, which required a series of tests and an inpatient stay of a few days. When I received the news, I was at a week-long conference in Boston, and I found some comfort in knowing that Sharon and their mother were there for her. Unfortunately, a day or two later, while I was at a black-tie event, Sharon called to inform me Deborah had fainted while walking down the hall and was being transferred to the ICU. Alarm shot through me: my sister was in trouble. An almost visceral need to jump into action all but overcame me, even though I didn't know the full details of Deborah's condition. In reality, there was very little I could do from Boston, and I knew it. Even still, I had to do something, so I left the ballroom in my tuxedo and found a quiet place to pray for her.

The next morning, we came together as a family on a conference call so we could speak with Deborah's team of nurses and physicians. At some point overnight, Deborah had been placed on an intra-aortic balloon pump to improve the flow of blood through the arteries that supplied her heart. Shockingly, we learned Deborah had needed a new heart for some time, even though she'd never once shared the gravity of her situation with us. (Later, after I'd broached the subject with her, I learned that she'd been privately struggling with all that a transplant would mean for her, her son, and the prospective donor's family.) As soon as I could get away from Boston, I flew to New Orleans to be with her. At the hospital, I found Deborah in the cardiac ICU hooked up to several IV lines that were distributing multiple medications through a central venous catheter; an arterial line measured her blood pressure from heartbeat to heartbeat. The glowing monitors around her displayed a range of complex vital-sign readings as they beeped. As a physician, scenes like this were all too familiar, yet now I was in an unfamiliar seat as a family member of a critically ill patient. As Deborah's brother, advocate, and a doctor now invited into her corner, I had to resign myself to the reality of my sister needing a new heart. Right then and there, I decided it was my job to work with her and her doctors to make that happen.

Deborah's clinical course over the next few days was stable, but she was unable to get out of bed because of the balloon pump and her tangle of IV lines. With her blessing, I returned to Chicago—grateful that other family members were still at her bedside—to help my wife and kids pack for a business trip they were joining me on the following week. Knowing it would soon be time for Deborah to start having more concrete discussions with her doctors about her options, I reached out to Howard alumni who'd gone on to sub-specialize in cardiothoracic surgery. They gave me some excellent information and a list of questions: Could Deborah get on the heart-transplant list? Which treatments could manage her condition, even if only in the short term? What immediate steps could she take to improve her quality of life? I passed the list on to Deborah. Her doctors told her she needed further tests and time to build up her strength before she would be eligible for the transplant list. (Patients must meet strict criteria before they can become transplant candidates.) As a temporizing step to overcoming her congestive heart failure, her doctors suggested she have a left ventricular assist device (LVAD) placed. As the name implies, this electronic device is surgically attached to the heart and uses a small but sophisticated pump that essentially replaces the pumping action of the heart's left ventricle. This ensures oxygenated blood gets circulated to the heart's arteries, the brain, and all other vital organs. The LVAD would serve as a bridge to a future transplant, and successful placement would give her back some control of her life. However, LVADs were (and still are) a big deal, and the only way to place one was via a lengthy open-heart surgery that carried many risks—from internal bleeding to a stroke, to death. Beyond that, the pump, once inserted, requires constant electrical power from rechargeable batteries. These batteries are worn outside the body and connect to the LVAD via a semipermanent cord that travels through the abdominal wall and into the chest. Living with an LVAD would be a major adjustment for my sister, but there was no easy answer, no single solution, and no risk-free move to make. I voiced my own thoughts on the matter while knowing the decision was ultimately up to her.

Two days later, as my family and I were boarding our flight at O'Hare, Deborah called. She'd decided to have the LVAD placed, and—much to my disbelief—she was heading into the operating room as we spoke. I knew how beneficial the device could be for her health, yet I almost couldn't process the moment itself: here I was, buckling into my seat and about to fly 4,000 miles even further away from my sister, while Deborah was being wheeled into an operating room in

New Orleans. I prayed to God, asking Him to bless the hands of the surgeons who would be operating on her.

Mentally, this was the most agonizing flight of my life. Powerless to connect with Deborah's surgeons or even be in the waiting room, my entire flight was filled with uncertainty. Shawn understood my anxiety, and she too prayed for Deborah and our family while attesting to the promise of God's grace and mercy. My wife didn't allow me to dwell on the disturbing thoughts filling my mind, and she helped me focus on the likelihood that Deborah's future would be brighter very soon. That calmed me, but it didn't take away my dread completely—when the plane landed, I would still have to turn my phone back on and face whatever reality was waiting for me. A single text or voicemail message could either break my heart or imbue me with hope.

We touched down in Honolulu and while walking through the jet bridge with my two sons in tow, I checked my voicemail, not realizing that this wasn't the best place to do so since I could upset my boys if the news were unfortunate. I swiped at my phone's screen and saw the new-voicemail icon was lit up. I braced myself for the worst, but thankfully Deborah came out of the lengthy surgery without complications. I thanked God—a long list of things could have gone wrong in the operating room, but He had spared my sister of any in-surgery setbacks. Especially heartening was that Deborah no longer needed her intra-aortic balloon pump, and it had been removed without issue. The tension and fear in my body dissipated as I breathed a huge sigh of relief.

With my heart gladdened, the next morning Shawn and I went to our conference, while the nanny and our boys enjoyed Honolulu's white-sand beaches. Hawai'i was beautiful beyond measure, and all the more so given Deborah's improving status. Within a few days, she was already on the mend and well enough to sit up in bed or walk over to the chair in her room. Our family rejoiced; we'd been afforded extra time with Deborah, and after a few weeks had passed, we practically cheered when she could walk without becoming short of breath. My gratefulness soared beyond measure: the Lord had given me the opportunity to counsel my sister through this trying time, and the bond between Deborah and I became all the stronger.

AFTER GRADUATING FROM SOUTHERN UNIVERSITY LAW CENTER IN BAton Rouge, Deborah had launched her career by working as a law clerk, but she later found her true passion in education. She taught at the college, vocational, and high school levels. Beloved by her students, she continually affirmed their ability to succeed while sharing her naturally positive outlook on life. As her health had declined, it became necessary for her to retire from teaching, but her students didn't forget her. During her home convalescence after her LVAD placement, many of her former students checked up on her regularly, as did her friends. In fact, Deborah became a kind of medical celebrity since few people in our hometown had LVADs. (At the time, LVADs weren't unknown to the public; former vice president Dick Cheney had had his implanted only a few years before.) My family and I knew the LVAD was only a stopgap to a heart transplant, but Deborah's quality of life was greatly improved, and when she learned Anthony and his girlfriend were pregnant, no one was more ecstatic. She was so looking forward to becoming a grandmother that it motivated her to keep up with the diet and exercise routines recommended by her cardiologists.

As Deborah began working up the courage to become a transplant candidate, her life now included regular trips to see her cardiology team in New Orleans. Unfortunately, within a year, we learned that her kidneys were at risk of failing; to avoid dialysis in the future, she needed a kidney transplant. I knew it wasn't uncommon for diabetes to debilitate kidney function over time, but the news revealed yet another health challenge for my sister, one that we would all have to bear together as a family. And now that Deborah needed a kidney in addition to a heart, she had to transfer her care from New Orleans to another transplant program in Dallas. While the distance from Shreveport to Dallas is much shorter than to New Orleans, switching her care meant leaving behind the cardiac team who we'd built a trusting relationship with and essentially starting over.

In the summer of 2015, I had several conversations with Deborah's Dallas-based cardiologist about care plans going forward. So far, it had been a good summer: despite her timid kidney function, Deborah was losing weight healthfully and was feeling relatively well. Yet my heart sank as her doctor shared some disconcerting news: after reviewing her case, the transplant committee had determined Deborah was doing too well to be added to the heart-transplant list. They also decided that the risks of transplantation outweighed the benefits at that time. This felt odd to me since my sister didn't have a voice in the matter; why hadn't she been included in the risk-benefit conversation? Plus, even though Deborah was doing well, the fundamentals of her situation hadn't changed in my medical opinion; she still needed a new heart and would eventually need a new kidney. Waiting until she was critically ill to put her on the heart-transplant list didn't make sense to me.

At the end of the summer, her cardiologist and I had another physician-to-physician conversation. I still didn't see why my sister wasn't on the heart-transplant list, and I pushed hard to have her added while she was still strong. Her cardiologist told me that during the last transplant committee meeting, everyone except him had voted against adding Deborah to the list. He explained that the committee was made up of diverse healthcare professionals—physicians, nurses, coordinators, and others—and some of them were skeptical that Deborah would be compliant with her post-transplant regimen of anti-rejection medications. Others suspected she wouldn't follow the other requirements of her cardiac rehabilitation plan. These presumptions didn't make sense to me; Deborah always took her medications as prescribed and kept all her doctors' appointments. I made my case for her again, but the decision had already been made. When the call was over, I practically slammed down the phone. Where did this bias against my sister come from, and where was the medical team who was supposed to be in her corner? But more than anything else, I was disappointed in myself. I'd been her health advocate for years, but when Deborah really needed me to come through, I couldn't deliver. I'd done all I could to ensure she received the best care possible, yet I couldn't get her a new heart.

I'm not sure which qualities the transplant committee saw or didn't see in my sister. First and foremost, Deborah was a mother, grandmother, daughter, sister, aunt, and friend to many. She was an African American woman who overcame the odds and achieved a meaningful career as an educator. She was a first-generation college graduate who went on to earn a Doctorate in Jurisprudence. She was kind, considerate of others, generous, and her smile could brighten anyone's day. She wanted to live a healthy and vibrant life, and she was actively doing all she could to achieve that. All these traits, and many more, were invisible to the transplant committee. Yet there was one trait the committee could see clearly: her race. The healthcare system has a long, verifiable history of racial discrimination—I've seen examples of it with my own eyes—and I'm sure the color of Deborah's skin was a factor in the committee's decision. Whether it was unconscious bias or outright racism at play, the justifications for keeping her off the transplant list didn't make sense clinically, not even after I'd spoken to several cardiothoracic surgeons in my network.

Deborah remained in relatively good health over the next few months, during which time I explored future care options. Things were going well for her until an unexpected, slowly developed brain bleed put her back in the hospital. Cerebral hemorrhaging was an uncommon but possible complication of the blood thinners Deborah was taking to support her LVAD function. (Thinning the blood virtually eliminates the risk of small, potentially-artery-clogging blood clots developing due to the LVAD.) As she was being flown from Shreveport to Dallas, I tracked down the neurosurgeon who would be handling her case and called him to advocate for my sister. I then sprinted to O'Hare and hopped on the first available flight to Dallas. By the time I arrived at the hospital, Deborah was just coming out of the post-anesthesia care unit, and I was able to meet her in the ICU. The procedure was a success, but we were now entering new territory. Deborah knew this too, and I quietly held her hand while at her bedside.

Although her conditions were outside of my specialty, it was clear to me Deborah couldn't go back on blood thinners, at least not right after her brain surgery. This was risky, though, as removing the risk of bleeding could open the door to the risk of clotting. When I talked to her cardiology team, their assessment was the same: use of blood thinners posed a greater, and even life-threatening, risk than any potential LVAD-related blood clots. This was certainly bad news, yet even more ominous were the implications for Deborah's potential transplant. Not being one to give up, I'd spent the last few months gearing up for another battle with a transplant committee, but now my network of cardiothoracic surgeons told me that the door was officially closed to a transplant, as no surgeon would risk the likelihood of uncontrolled bleeding in the brain during an organ transplant. (Blood thinners are an essential part of heart transplantation. During the moments when a diseased heart is removed from the chest cavity and the donor heart is being implanted, surgeons place the body's circulation system on a bypass machine to keep vital organs supplied with oxygenated blood. However, much like an LVAD, a bypass machine can cause small clots to develop if the blood is not properly thinned.) With blood thinners now contraindicated for Deborah, her already-slim chances of becoming a heart-transplant candidate were gone.

I thought we had more time to fight for a heart transplant, but the advocacy clock had silently run down. Deborah had even worked up the courage for such a major procedure, but now the LVAD—which was always intended to be temporary—became her definitive therapy. Fortunately, she recovered well from the brain bleed, and after a short stay in a rehabilitation facility, she was sent home. Over the next few months, she returned to making steady progress. Yet in an unexpected turn, she contracted a healthcare-associated infection. Somewhere during the course of her inpatient stays and outpatient visits, her LVAD became contaminated with pseudomonas aeruginosa, a bacterium notoriously resistant to most antibiotics. Unfortunately, this led to intermittent hospital stays over the next few months. With this latest complication now in the mix, it became clear that her medical team in Dallas was not overly interested in her care. During her last hospitalization, my family and I determined that Deborah was receiving inadequate support, and she decided to transfer her care back to her team in New Orleans. It was Christmastime 2015 when she was ready to be discharged from the hospital in Dallas. Our usual flight to Louisiana for the holidays included a layover in Dallas, so we decided to end our flight there and drive Deborah home for Christmas. We rented a Chevy Suburban at the airport and picked up my sister at the hospital. As I carefully piloted us on the three-hour drive to Shreveport, Deborah sang songs with the boys for most of the ride.

With a failing heart and an ongoing, drug-resistant infection, we were backed into a corner. Her doctors prescribed continued intravenous antibiotics at home, and whenever her health took a dip, she went back to New Orleans for care. Later, when her heart function started worsening, her care team added a dobutamine continuous infusion (a drug for severe heart failure) into her intravenous regimen. Yet her heart continued to grow worse over the next six months. Almost every day, I asked myself what would've happened if I'd been successful in getting my sister on the heart-transplant list during the summer when she'd been judged to be too well. Should I have made more phone calls, written an Op-Ed about systemic racism in healthcare? Camped outside the transplant director's office?

Even given her progressing illness, Deborah still enjoyed some good times, including quality time with family and her grandchild, fishing in the back yard with our dad, and taking part in a local American Heart Association fundraising event. Moments like these kept her going. Yet as the months rolled on, her antibiotics became less effective in fighting her infection. With the antibiotics not working optimally, her infection spread to her bloodstream, resulting in septic shock. She needed even more antibiotics to treat her sepsis, and these powerful drugs severely harmed her fragile kidneys, forcing her to start dialysis. With this bevy of comorbidities to manage, Deborah was essentially living to fight illness rather than actually living her life.

Even though Deborah had fought the good fight, we knew her time on Earth was drawing to its close. There were no viable options that would cure her conditions and give her the quality of life she desired. She had made it clear to me that if she ever reached this point, she didn't want to suffer needlessly and hopelessly. I gathered our family on the phone on a Saturday morning, and although we all knew Deborah's wishes, that knowledge didn't make our reality easier to accept. After we all spoke that morning, my family and I were of one accord. I then made a difficult call to her cardiologist to provide the family's consent to withdraw care—Deborah needed her rest and her peace. On Saturday, December 3rd, 2016, she passed away with her mom and sisters at her side.

My being a doctor wasn't enough to save my own sister's life. In my mind, I hadn't trained to lose this battle; as far as I was concerned, the healthcare system was supposed to work, yet it had failed to work for Deborah—and the rest of us. Even with my medical study and years of training, all my state and local advocacy work, and my decade in practice, in the end, the best I could do was be there as part of the family who loved, cared for, and—in her last days—made sure she transitioned from this life with dignity and surrounded by our love. I found the greatest comfort in knowing that she was no longer suffering, but Deborah's absence left a huge hole in our hearts. In the days and weeks after her passing, I struggled to find the peace that comes from accepting only God truly is in control, although I was eventually able to surrender to His wisdom. At the same time, though, I vowed that the next time my family and I faced a health crisis, I would be a better advocate and fight harder and smarter.

CHAPTER 17

Mentoring: Giving Back is Good for the Soul

THROUGH THE STORIES MY MOTHER TOLD ME ABOUT OUR FAMILY MEMbers, I learned early on that no one is put on this Earth solely for their own benefit. We have so much to share with each other, and we can enrich each other in so many ways. I stored my mom's lessons like mini-instruction books in my mind and called on them to help guide my day-to-day decisions, especially in instances when my innate, immature instincts or lack of life experience temped me down paths that would've very likely led me to the wrong places. Because my mom offered me her wisdom so freely, I always felt comfortable approaching others in my family and community for counsel. They too were generous. As I came into my own as a young man, it came time for me to be generous to those coming up behind me.

Not long after starting my freshman year of college, I joined a mentoring program called Mobilization at Xavier (MAX), which connected students at Xavier with New Orleans schools. I was assigned to Lafayette Elementary, a school that was a fifteen-minute walk from campus.

My role was to foster literacy by reading aloud to children in the first and second grades. I don't really remember the books I read to them, but I do remember the smiles on the kids' faces at story time. I'd joined MAX mainly because Xavier encouraged first-year students to begin accumulating community-service-hour-credits from day one and also because I wanted to get to know the community beyond our campus, but my time with these kids cemented the responsibility I had to the next generation.

Later on, after I'd joined Kappa Alpha Psi, my chapter chose James Lewis Elementary as the primary partner for its Guide Right National Service Program. This school was further from campus than Lafayette Elementary in a well-to-do neighborhood called Uptown. However, most of the kids attending James Lewis, a public school, were Black and African American students from poorer neighborhoods. At first glance, the school's mentoring program seemed well supported—a few retired lawyers and other professionals were volunteers—but when I looked more closely, I realized very few looked like me or my fraternity brothers. I knew I could make a difference here.

At James Lewis, we worked with boys in the fifth grade, visiting with them weekly on Wednesdays for an hour. The teachers literally turned their students over to us, and it was up to us to make our visit a valuable experience for them. Although our time with the kids flew by each week, my fraternity brothers and I saw ourselves in these soon-to-be young men. Collectively, we understood the neighborhood violence that so many of them faced: how poverty and low expectations threatened to place a ceiling on their potential; how, for so many of them, unrest and instability shaped their outlooks on life. The obstacles these children faced were high, and each week we poured into them all the wisdom we could impart. These kids were our little brothers: we wanted them to know we were betting on their success. We challenged them to reach new levels of self-respect and academic achievement, and we encouraged them to set positive goals for themselves. Our hope was that they could see themselves in us, see us pursuing dreams that so many of them had never considered or even thought possible. We represented a tangible path forward, one that few of them had seen in their home lives. Yet as much as we gave to these students, they gave back to us tenfold: guiding them and inspiring them nurtured our hearts.

During the final semester of my senior year in 1998, as I was completing my term as Kappa Alpha Psi's undergraduate vice president for the Southwestern Province, I hosted a career-networking seminar at our council meeting in Houston. My vision was inspired by the belief that connecting current Kappas with Kappa alumni would elevate the success of our undergraduates. We paired every student at the seminar with a mentor, with the goal of increasing our undergraduates' chances of acceptance into graduate/professional schools or securing successful job placements post-graduation. The event was a success, and it even caught the attention of the fraternity's leadership on the national level. My hope was that this effort would continue, and the incoming undergraduate vice president John A. Kuykendall, III, made sure the event was repeated the following year.

I continued mentoring while in medical school, where, through our student council program, I helped organize mentoring events for youth in the greater DC area. It was then that I learned, through a good friend of mine who was a middle-school teacher in Maryland, about the challenges his tween and teen students were facing with sexually transmitted infections. As a doctor-to-be, I knew I could help, and around 2000, with the assistance of my classmates Carla Burks-Wicks and Sean Frederick, I developed a program on sexual health and disease prevention that I targeted specifically to these budding young adults. We started our program at Benjamin Banneker High School in DC, where we were welcomed with open arms as a supplement to the school's own sexual health efforts. As medical students preparing to enter our clinical years, this was a great training opportunity for us, but more importantly, we knew that we were influencing the choices these young people were making through both the information we shared and by our presence. In my own young life, there had been many moments when the wisdom and guidance shared with me had left an indelible influence on me, and I knew in my soul that I had created such moments for these young people.

Around the same time, my classmate and I grew our team of medical-student volunteers and began hosting classes of students from a Maryland middle-school mentoring program called Kings and Queens. When these students visited campus, we presented our sexual health program in one of Howard's lecture halls, and we also took them on small group tours through the medical school. Of course, the gross anatomy lab was always on the list of places students wanted to visit, and while we were happy to oblige their curiosity, we also imparted to them the sacred esteem in which we, as medical students, held for the lab: our teachers in the lab—the cadavers—had shared themselves with us after their deaths so that we could learn and become physicians.

Our efforts with these middle and high school students were foundational to the development of a new model for youth education, which was spearheaded by my classmate, Ernest Brown. His vision was to create student-led videos that could aid in reducing the transmission of HIV. A small group of us worked together on a proposal entitled "Creating a Peer-Guided AIDS Education Video Program." We submitted the paper to the 2000–2001 competition for the U.S. Department of Health and Human Services' Secretary's Award for Innovations in Health Promotion and Disease Prevention. It was an honor to receive the second-place award from HHS Secretary Tommy G. Thompson.

When I moved to Chicago for residency, it was the beginning of an exciting but time-consuming period in my career that required me to focus my efforts narrowly on medicine, although I didn't stay out of the mentoring game for long. During the fall of 2004, at the start of my third residency year, grand polemarch Samuel C. Hamilton, Kappa Alpha Psi's national president, called me one evening. I knew brother Hamilton well; over the years, I'd gotten to know him and his humble, dignified leadership style. He had a new vision for encouraging undergraduate Kappa men to go to graduate/professional schools across the nation. He wanted me to step forward, build on legacy efforts in the health professions, and lead a new initiative that would be known as the Achievement Academy.

There I was in the last year of my residency, preparing to apply to business schools, and already serving as a national officer for the EMRA. My plate was full, but I was drawn to brother Hamilton's vision: I could make space to lead this effort, and I knew I had an incredible network of high-achieving leaders that I could tap for support. When I took on the role as chairman of the Academy's advisory committee, I was the most junior national committee chairman in the fraternity, but the early efforts of the Academy wouldn't have been successful without the strong partnerships of Dr. Jerlando F. L. Jackson, Dr. Terry Esper, Dr. John A. Kuykendall, III, Dr. Charles H. F. Davis, III, Steven J.

Pritchett, Esq. and Dr. Anthony F. Powell. We formed cohorts centered around a professional/graduate school discipline, each of which was led by a national chairperson, and we tailored the program within each cohort so that our young Kappas received more targeted support.

As a committee, we had a lot going for us. Not only were we well-placed within our respective areas of expertise, but we had all the energy and drive of young men still in our twenties and thirties. We worked passionately to recruit a national base of mentors in the areas of business, education, engineering, social sciences, and humanities, and we worked just as hard in encouraging our undergraduate members to attend Academy seminars. The Academy's programs covered the basics of undergraduate academic excellence, internship opportunities, demystifying standardized tests, applying to graduate or professional schools, and the importance of networking. At the regional level, we held in-person mentoring events each fall and spring. Over the years, we supported hundreds of young men as they advanced toward their professional lives.

I worked with the Achievement Academy until 2011. That year was the fraternity's centennial, and the celebration drew in one of our largest-ever meetings for the Academy. 2011 was also the year I became a father, and although I was proud to bring my baby son to his very first fraternity meeting, I needed to shift some of my focus onto parenting. With Kappa Alpha Psi going one hundred years strong, and with so many talented, dedicated men still on the committee, this was a good year for me to turn the Achievement Academy over to a new leader; with both pride and gratitude, I stepped down as chairman.

～

THROUGHOUT MY SERVICE TO THE ACHIEVEMENT ACADEMY, I HAD been doing double duty in the mentoring world. As a member of Kappa Alpha Psi's Chicago Alumni Chapter, in 2004 I was introduced to a small mentoring program led by our member Rodney Gore. This program was a part of the fraternity's national Kappa League program, and it would soon be locally branded as the Kappa Leadership Institute Chicago (KLIC). This program for male teens hit all the traditional mentoring notes of college prep support, but in many ways, it pushed its young men even further. After only a few site visits, I was hooked on the energy, vitality, and uniqueness of KLIC and the enrolled Kappa Leaguers, and as my residency training ended, I committed to serve as the KLIC's co-leader.

While the KLIC was open to all high school males, it predominantly attracted Black and Latino students. We aimed to empower the young men in our communities to realize their dreams, overcome the statistics that were stacked against them, and have a positive-multiplier effect over the years. To prepare our Kappa Leaguers for college, at our biweekly afterschool meetings we taught them leadership principles, standardized-exam preparation, and writing skills. We believed that higher education was key to the future success of program participants, and so, to remove or alleviate the financial barriers to higher education, we worked to position them as candidates for scholarships. But perhaps most importantly of all, we demanded that Kappa Leaguers comport themselves with equal parts self-respect and respect for others.

Before I was involved with the KLIC, there were fewer than thirty students enrolled. After just a few years under my leadership, our numbers soared to nearly one hundred students from more than thirty high schools across the Chicagoland area. The support KLIC received from our fraternity brothers was strong, but to maintain our quality, as the program scaled up (and to fill some gaps in various areas of expertise), we brought in mentors from other fraternities alongside tutors (both male and female) to assist our young men with their learning. With a sense of urgency, to increase Kappa Leaguer success, we formed partnerships with colleges and universities across the Midwest and across the nation. Our mission soon grew bigger than fraternal identity; it was a positive, empowering force for young men for whom too many had set low expectations.

A highlight of the KLIC, especially in its early years, was the college tour program. Most students could tour Chicago's many colleges and universities themselves, but for some, Chicagoland was the only region they were able to access on their own. Our annual program brought Kappa Leaguers to various regions of the country; over a four-year period, students visited schools all over the US, with a number of colleges available on each trip. And we didn't simply escort our young men on these tours: we prepared them in a whole-student-support way. Our prep sessions didn't merely include essay-writing and application assistance, but—with the care of elders in a village—we taught them how to present themselves and make good first impressions. We ensured that each young man owned a black suit, knew how to properly wear a tie, understood the importance of personal grooming, and developed strong verbal skills. This preparation occurred on a biweekly basis and the annual recognition of our success came when our students landed on college campuses for their tours and challenged the negative stereotypes that so many believed about them. By taking a whole-student approach, we were able to give each of our Kappa Leaguers exactly what he needed, in the very form in which he needed it. One former mentee of mine, a young man named Daniel Hernandez, recently told me, "You found a way to speak to me that was relatable yet professional while your presence also commanded respect. In every interaction we had, you held me accountable—whether that be fixing my tie or raising my grades in school. Your presence [at KLIC], reliability, and advice is what pushed me to go to Howard."

In time, we became a regular feeder of students to the Posse Foundation scholarship program, and in the same vein, several of our students became Gates Millennium Scholarship Program recipients. We partnered with local programs like Chicago Scholars to lend our students greater access to early, onsite admissions-programs for colleges. To strengthen our performance and efficiency, KLIC used an online portal system to better engage with teachers, counselors, and parents throughout the year and especially during the college application process.

The portal was one means through which we held our young men accountable at the individual level, but we also practiced group accountability and encouraged our students to support each other whenever and however they could. One year, when a student was late in submitting his essay for my review, I found out that the issue was a lack of Internet in the home. I brought the student to my house to use my computer, then in the next KLIC meeting, I told my approximately fifteen senior students that, as a whole, they didn't meet the deadline for submitting college applications to me. I asked them if they had reached out to their fellow seniors and offered each other help with any barriers. They spent the next twenty minutes talking to each other and eventually discovered that they had left someone behind. Right then, as a class, they pledged they would all make it to the finish line together.

Our numbers proved the success of our whole-student approach. In the years 2005–2008:

- 100% of our students matriculated to college.
- 96% were in the top 15% of their class.
- More than 8 in 10 had a GPA above 3.4.
- 63% of seniors received a full scholarship offer.
- In 2008 specifically, our average ACT score was 28 (out of 34).

Kappa Leaguers' successes were hard-won, especially given their starting points.

In 2008:

- 32% entered the program with less than a 2.5 GPA.
- 78% lived in a single-parent household primarily headed by a woman.
- 63% had had no contact with their biological father in over three years.
- 72% would be the first in their family to attend college.
- 54% resided in a home where the total household income was less than $48,000 annually.
- 57% lived in an area that they considered "violent or unsafe."
- 28% had been diagnosed with a reading or other learning disability and/or ADHD.

While we enjoyed college matriculation rates nearing one hundred percent, we learned that our students needed more support around thriving on college campuses that looked and felt very different from the west and south sides of Chicago. To help our alumni, during semester breaks and long weekends, we brought together our graduates. They shared their experiences with each other, helped their fellow alumni with challenges, and celebrated their successes. We also introduced them to our current Kappa Leaguers, which our alumni found very inspiring and looked forward to at every turn. Meeting current Kappa Leaguers was so popular that, regularly enough, alumni would drop into KLIC meetings if they happened to be home from college.

Especially for our students who matriculated to more affluent colleges and universities, a common point of feedback was that they often felt out of place. Unlike some of their more privileged undergraduate classmates, our young men didn't have family vacation homes, and many hadn't traveled outside the U.S. In fact, our college tours were the first time that many of our young men had left Chicagoland, and for some, our west-coast college tour was their first trip on an airplane. Gaps like these made many an alum feel like a fish out of water, which of course threatened to impede their educational success. KLIC knew of the problem, but we didn't know what could be done until Rodney came up with the radical idea of adding a study-abroad component to our program during the summer. We partnered with the American Field Service Intercultural Program USA (AFS-USA) to make this happen, although getting the program off the ground was quite a feat. We had to contend with challenges like parental apprehension, students' fears of being away from home and/or flying, lack of passports among students, and basic language lessons for students going to non-English-speaking countries. Issues like these were just the tip of the iceberg, plus we had to provide financial support for our Kappa Leaguers so that the cost of travel wouldn't be prohibitive or a financial burden. That first year took a lot of work, but Rodney and I were relentless in our efforts to make this vision a reality because it held such promise for our young men.

With AFS-USA funding us, we pulled it off. The foundation made resources available for our students, and with a lot of work, we were able to get our first study abroad cohort away for the summer and back home safely. For many of these young men, and for many more in the years to come, the trip was transformative. Parents consistently noted that their sons were more mature, grateful, and independent following their study abroad experience. Many of our students began using their trip abroad as material for their college-application essays and/or college interview discussions. The program was such a resounding success that we decided to make study abroad with KLIC mandatory for students during the summer between their junior and senior years of high school. This brought its own set of challenges: we had to intensify our exam-prep programming to ensure that students were hitting their SAT and ACT marks before the summer started, and we had to make certain that they—well before the close of their junior year—were working with their counselors to gather letters of recommendation and transcripts. They had to stay ahead of the game on these tasks since they would return only a few short weeks before the start of their senior year and the beginning of our accelerated college-application process.

Beyond college readiness, we also had a community obligation to prepare our Kappa Leaguers for adult life. Since KLIC attracted mostly Black and Brown young men, we knew they needed the skills to overcome the current and future inequities of life. From law enforcement to education, medicine to engineering, business to law, we were never short on practical life lessons to share with our students. But we were only successful because our young men were open to that success; with few exceptions, our Kappa Leaguers were coachable, open-minded, motivated, disciplined, and willing to make mistakes and learn from them. It was, quite literally, a winning combination. In 2009, our efforts were recognized on the national level by Kappa Alpha Psi when we were awarded the Jay Crosby Award. This award, which recognizes the fraternity's most outstanding Guide Right or community service program in the nation, is only given biennially, making it that much more of an honor.

In my ten-year affiliation with the KLIC, we influenced the lives of more than nine hundred young men who have gone on to be achievers in many fields, and I'm proud to have been a part of their journey. For many of them, success wasn't a straight shot to the finish line; some stumbled, others faced sabotage, and some made mistakes along the way. But because they were part of a community that cared for and believed in them, they always made their way back into the game. The young men of KLIC, with their spirit and ambition, have truly been some of my greatest teachers, and they helped shape me into a better man, better husband, better father, and better leader. KLIC has been one of the greatest instances of mentoring in my life and will always remain close to my heart.

As my corporate responsibilities increased and my sons grew older, I stepped back from my leadership role with KLIC in 2015 to make room for others to step up, and to provide my sons with the increased attention they needed as grade-schoolers. Since then, I have seen our Kappa Leaguers graduate from universities across the country. Many continued onto graduate schools and earned degrees in divinity, business, engineering, medicine, law, art—the list goes on. One summer while traveling to New York City, I bumped into a KLIC student outside of the terminal at LaGuardia airport as he was traveling out of the country for his study abroad program. It was heartening to see the KLIC continuing its impact and sending our young men around the world as ambassadors of Chicago. Sometimes it really does take a village, and that village for so many young Chicagoans is KLIC.

CHAPTER 18

Native Sons

RAISING TWO SONS HAS BEEN BOTH AN EXCITING JOURNEY AND ONE filled with sacred responsibility. African American males have historically and contemporarily faced systemic racism, low scholastic expectations, higher rates of discipline in school, over-policing, mass incarceration, gun violence, and shorter life expectancies than their peers. As a father, I'm charged with changing these societal predestinations for my sons and insulating them from the false stereotypes that could discourage them and blunt their potential. Truthfully, I know that I won't succeed alone, but I have faith in God, the progress of our community, our village of family and friends, and the wisdom imparted to me over the years by my elders and mentors.

In the first decade of being a father, I have experienced moments of immense pride and agonized over incredible disappointment. Unlike those of prior generations, my sons grew up seeing, during their formative years, an African American president of the United States: a Black man in the White House is a perfectly normal occurrence in their worldview. Despite this remarkable marker of progress in American politics, my job is to prepare my sons for the real world that awaits them. This means ensuring that they form a strong sense of history and understand the racial and cultural journey of America's quest to become a more just and perfect union. With resilience and vision, my boys can hopefully someday supersede the accomplishments of those who came before them and keep the progress of our nation pushing forward.

Right up there with my pride in being a father has been the privilege of raising my sons with their loving mother and my wife, Shawn. As a pediatrician, children are the center of Shawn's professional world, and together we care for the two special blessings, Grant and Reid, that God placed in our lives. We believe in being proactive parents, and this means supporting our boys in as many ways as we possibly can. To supplement our focus on history and education, it's been our practice to flood the reading zone in our home with books, and our boys have hundreds of them in their bedrooms. In fact, their first collection of books was a gift from our friend Chrissie whose selections included books with images of children who look like them as well as children from various cultures around the world. As parents, we have always placed a special focus on finding children's books that tell the true stories of our nation's beginnings, including the exploitation and mistreatment of Native Americans and the bondage African Americans endured for centuries. We've read to them about the Civil Rights Movement, and we intentionally and age-appropriately talk with them about contemporary issues of social inequity. We want our sons educated about the society in which they live; when it comes time for them to go out in the world, they'll be prepared.

As a supplement to our reading at home, beginning when the boys were ages five and seven, we began taking educational trips as a family to historic sites and landmarks. On our first trip, we visited the Whitney

Plantation, which is located just off the banks of the Mississippi River and is about halfway between New Orleans and Baton Rouge in my home state of Louisiana. There they gazed upward at a memorial granite wall that lists the African names of the enslaved who arrived in Louisiana on one side and the names they were given by their owners on the other. When the boys stood next to clay sculptures of slave children their size, they learned that children suffered slavery as well. As we walked in the hot sun, my oldest son rang the large plantation bell to give voice to his ancestors who were once controlled by its toll, and we touched the rusty hinges of steel cages that were once used in slave auctions. My family and I toured a slave cabin and walked through the detached kitchen where enslaved cooks prepared meals for their owner and his family. Inside the plantation's Big House, with its high ceilings and opulence, the children pointed out how unfair it was for the slave cabins to be so small.

When we brought the boys to the National Underground Railroad Freedom Center in Cincinnati, much to their surprise, there was no train on display. They had read stories about Harriet Tubman and the Underground Railroad, and although this network of escape routes, abolitionists, and hiding places didn't employ an actual train, Grant and Reid were expecting one, nonetheless. Drawn to the chains on display, my sons picked up shackles and cuffs that were used to keep slaves captive, and they speculated on how the enslaved might have broken free from their bonds. After reading the story of Henry "Box" Brown at his exhibit, the boys crawled inside a replica of the wooden crate Brown used to mail himself to freedom.[24] Outside, standing by

---

24 The National Park Service: <https://bit.ly/3F3JKXO>

the Freedom Center (which is adjacent to the north bank of the Ohio River), I pointed across the water as I explained to the boys that during the days of Harriet Tubman, the south side was where slavery existed while the north side where we stood was freedom.

On another trip, this one to historic Montgomery, we visited the National Memorial for Peace and Justice. A solemn and sober place, this memorial forced us to talk about America's history of racial inequality and the terror of lynching. The memorial is largely comprised of approximately eight hundred hanging steel rectangles, each bronze in color and roughly the size and shape of a coffin, arranged in seemingly never-ending rows. Each rectangle represents a US county where, between the years 1877–1950, someone was lynched, and each is engraved with the names of those who were lynched.[25] We eventually found the rectangle for my home parish of Caddo, where the last recorded lynching was in 1926,[26] and we gazed upward as I showed the boys the names of those lost to such deplorable violence. I took care to point out to the boys that one of their great-grandfathers was born in 1888; as a younger man, lynching was a real fear for him.

When we found the rectangles for counties in Illinois, I reminded the boys that lynching was not just a tragedy of the South. A plaque at the memorial noted, "Dozens of men, women, and children were lynched in a massacre in East St. Louis, Illinois, in 1917." Another memorialized William Donegan who, in 1908, was lynched in Springfield for having a white wife.[27] There are simply too many of these horrif-

---

25 The Equal Justice Initiative: <https://bit.ly/3ss3HTp>
26 America's Black Holocaust Museum: <https://bit.ly/3vX6lfb>
27 The Equal Justice Initiative: <https://bit.ly/3KBhMUq>

ic stories to document here, but a powerful quote engraved in black granite, which stands near the heart of the memorial, sums up why a visit to the National Memorial for Peace and Justice is such a profound educational and spiritual experience:

> For the hanged and beaten. For the shot, drowned, and burned. For the tortured, tormented, and terrorized. For those abandoned by the rule of law. We will remember. With hope because hopelessness is the enemy of justice. With courage because peace requires bravery. With persistence because justice is a constant struggle. With faith because we shall overcome.

It's never too early for children to be hopeful, courageous, and faithful, and we teach our sons that children can, in fact, make a difference. We often illustrate this by referring to the 1963 Children's Crusade, when more than one thousand children in Birmingham, Alabama from ages seven to eighteen peacefully protested racial injustice by marching from the Sixth Street Baptist Church to downtown Birmingham.[28] To help our sons understand the impact of this historic march, on the fifty-fifth anniversary of the Crusade, the four of us went to Birmingham to march the Crusade's route with other families from across the nation. The boys were particularly excited about this trip because of the historical importance, and we revisited pictures from our family trip to the Martin Luther King, Jr. Memorial in DC. Following the march, my oldest son met Martin Luther King, III, son of Dr. Martin Luther King, Jr., and both boys had a chance to hear the granddaugh-

---

28 The National Museum of African American History & Culture: <https://s.si.edu/37Vt-vzW>

ter of Dr. King, Yolanda R. King, speak at the Sixteenth Street Baptist Church, where, in September 1963, the Ku Klux Klan detonated a bomb that killed four young girls.[29] Ms. King spoke about her dream for a gun-free nation and her belief that today's young people could be a great generation and harbinger of change. Her eloquence and bravery in front of such a large audience was inspiring to my sons, the other children in the audience, and the adults alike.

We've taken the boys on a number of other trips as well, including to New Orleans, where they could learn about my Louisiana heritage and Mardi Gras culture. For our family, Mardi Gras has always been a family-friendly multicultural celebration, and it was our tradition to go yearly until the COVID-19 pandemic hit. The first time Grant figured out how to escape his pack-and-play crib we were in New Orleans for the carnival celebration. Over the years, I watched the boys learn how to dance to the soulful rhythms of New Orleans bands. As soon as they were old enough, during the parade, I would balance them on my shoulders so they could catch Mardi Gras beads from passing floats. In the years just before we had to pause our trips, the boys joined us for the early morning walk to the Zulu parade route on Fat Tuesday, where we marveled at the Mardi Gras Indians in their magnificent costumes. These elaborate, plumed-and-beaded costumes reflect a local blending of Native American and African cultures dating back hundreds of years.

There is truly a unique inspiration and sobering responsibility at the core of being a father, parent, or parental figure, and never had I imagined that my first few years of fatherhood would include the many

---

29 The National Park Service: <https://bit.ly/3MI84kS>

lessons that we learned together as a family. It would be impossible to document how much I've learned since my sons came into the world, and I'm sure there is much more to learn still. Fatherhood is hard to describe, impossible to perfect, and yet worthy of my best efforts. With Shawn by my side, I'll keep growing, evolving, and adapting to meet my sons' needs as they become young men.

WHILE I HAVE ALWAYS BEEN INTERESTED IN POLITICS, I'VE MADE A SPE-cial effort to refrain from steering my boys toward any one particular political party or ideology. My focus is on instilling the right values in them; from there, I trust Grant and Reid will make decisions that are right for them. Naturally, kids are interested in what their parents are watching, and to this end, my initial efforts to shield them involved curtailing my daily viewing habits of the evening news. That didn't work for long. During the 2016 presidential election, which pitted Hilary Clinton against Donald J. Trump, it became clear to me that even in elementary school, students were having political discussions. It wasn't uncommon for Grant, as young as he was, to come home with a perspective on the latest happenings in the campaign. Even though I felt one candidate was clearly dishonorable, I found myself steering Grant towards neutral and respectful discussions. Especially overconfident for a five-year-old child, he was convinced that he knew more about the election than I did, and when he accused one leading candidate of cheating, he believed that he didn't have to explain him-self—Dad just needed to believe him. "Out of the mouths of babes," I thought.

While I do my best not to influence my sons' nascent political views, when Barack Obama announced that his last public speaking engagement as president would be in Chicago at the McCormick Place Convention Center, I asked my oldest son if he wanted to attend with me. He gave me a resounding yes. Just after 4:00 a.m. on January 7th, 2017, Grant and I awoke on a cold Chicago morning and put on three layers of pants and shirts and two pairs of socks, and we continued bundling up from there. With our backpacks, hats, scarfs, coats, gloves, and hand warmers, we made the short trip to the convention center, where, at 5:00 a.m. we joined thousands of people in line for tickets to the president's speech. The morning's bitter cold made the experience that much more memorable, and Grant and I played an improvised game of "survivor" where each of us encouraged the other not to tap out. As the sun came up later in the morning, the length of the line became even more discouraging as it seemed like it never got any shorter. When the line finally made it near the Hyatt hotel, some incredibly nice people allowed us to jump out of line so I could grab some hot chocolate and warm up my son in the lobby. By 8:15 a.m., we were within twenty-five yards of the entrance to McCormick Place when rumors about all the tickets being gone began to circulate. Grant had reached his limit and began crying because he was freezing, but we were too close to bail out. Once inside the convention center, the line—still with at least five hundred people in it—zigzagged across the lobby: we were in the home stretch. Grant dried his eyes as I put a video on his tablet for him to watch, and my body began to thaw out after being outdoors. We waited for about one more hour. Then, at long last, at 9:46 a.m. we had our coveted tickets in hand for Obama's farewell address.

When we returned on January 10th, the lines were equally long, but thankfully we were waiting inside and there was no crying. It was a bittersweet evening of reflection for me. I remembered well the morning of November 4th, 2008, when the polls for the McCain/Obama presidential election first opened. Hope for Obama's victory seemed to fill our nation throughout the day, and I remembered the joy and awe felt by many Americans when this historic election was called at around 11:00 p.m. that evening. Two sons later, it was hard to see that era coming to an end, but watching President Obama give his farewell address was perhaps my first solo, daddy-and-son event with Grant, and historic it was.

Parents of African American sons live in a constant and very specific state of concern for their children's safety and well-being. As the boys grew, I knew the day when I would have to have the "Black male in America" talk was drawing near, although I admit that I deferred this for as long as I feasibly could. When I sat Grant and Reid down, it crushed my spirit to reveal that the institutionalized racism of our society means that, too often (and unlike their white peers), they will not be given the benefit of the doubt when trouble is afoot. It was torture to explain to them that, even after decades of social progress, bias and racism are still prevalent. For no other reason than the color of their skin, they can be treated differently from their peers. As a father, it's my job to tell them this truth, even as I actively work to keep stereotypes and bias as far from my sons as humanly possible.

During the hot summer months of 2020, Grant and Reid longed to get outside and play despite the lockdowns from the COVID-19 pandemic. To get them some fresh air and exercise, we often visited the baseball diamonds in Chicago's Grant Park, a wide-open space where social distancing was easily possible. Day after day, equal to their questions about going out to play were their curiosities about the caravans of police vehicles, with their lights and sirens, that passed through our neighborhood periodically. One afternoon, as I started my explanation about the ongoing Black Lives Matter protests, I told them that while riding our bikes to the park we needed to stay together and not get separated. I warned them that there was a chance we might run into large crowds of people or police, and regardless of what happened, we needed to stay together for safety. I knew that protests could at times become volatile, and I knew how mercilessly African American protestors have been treated in many instances. Even though we were just going to the park, precautions were necessary.

The boys knew why so many were protesting that summer. Culminating with the May 2020 murder of George Floyd, the repeated trauma of Black Americans being murdered at the hands of police became too much for our nation to bear in the midst of a pandemic that was out of control. Not that these killings were a new phenomenon, but the twenty-first century's technology, with video cameras on every smartphone and police routinely wearing body cams, increased visibility of these atrocities; no longer were such murders the stuff of speculation or oral history. Such vivid, violent, and heart-wrenching scenes forced Americans to confront the systemic racism in our society that even today still results in death. Across the summer, the citizens of Chicago—just like citizens in other cities large and small—were marching and protesting under the Black Lives Matter banner. For the most part, the nationwide protests were peaceful enough, but the sheer number of people marching through the streets shut down any number of major roadways and drew national media attention.

My boys had already heard some of the victims' names—Black Americans slain by police:

- Rayshard Brooks
- George Floyd
- Eric Garner
- Botham Jean
- Atatiana Jefferson
- Elijah McClain
- Laquan McDonald
- Daniel Prude
- Breonna Taylor

To my knowledge, the boys hadn't seen video clips of any of the murders (some of which were widely available on the Internet), but we couldn't hide the images of millions protesting around the nation. "Who was George Floyd and why did he die?" "Why are people mad at the police?" "Who was Laquan McDonald?" they asked. Shawn and I did our best to answer their questions, even though we didn't really have all the answers ourselves.

When raising Black sons, one huge challenge is fostering a positive—yet realistic and practical—view of law enforcement. With so many of our people grieving for those who died at the hands of the police, it would be much too easy to teach my boys that all cops are bad, when in reality, there are hundreds of thousands of police officers all over the nation who honor their oath, in word and deed, to protect and serve. When Grant had his COVID-19 lockdown birthday, several of our close friends with the Chicago Police Department led a surprise motorcade past our house with lights flashing and sirens blaring to wish him a happy birthday. This wasn't the first time Grant and Reid had seen, with their own eyes, love and respect from police officers they knew; until the protests began, they had ascribed that same credibility to all police officers. Yet after the excitement from the motorcade wore off, both my sons started asking questions about which officers were good and which ones were bad.

The conversation was a delicate one, and I had the primary focus of ensuring that Grant and Reid had a perspective and playbook that would keep them alive and safe, no matter the circumstances. Over the course of an hour, we sat in the living room and revisited both our family history and the historic sites to which we had traveled. We viewed photos and videos from the Whitney Plantation, The National Memorial for Peace and Justice, the National Underground Railroad Freedom Center, the Sixteenth Street Baptist Church, the National Museum of African American History and Culture, and the National Civil Rights Museum at the Lorraine Motel. We reflected on our participation in the fifty-fifth anniversary of the Children's Crusade, and we discussed why their local Jack and Jill chapter annually celebrates the life of Carole Robertson. Shawn and I delicately weaved together the struggles of our past to teach our sons about the challenges of today.

As we talked, I emphasized the reasons why our at-home lessons about integrity, excellence, listening, and respect are even more important to follow when outside the home. There is a time and place for everything, which means that my boys will need to discern, for their own survival, when to quiet their tongues, tempers, and righteous contempt when dealing with the police—or even with strangers on the street. We role-played a number of different scenarios so they will be prepared when I'm not around. With the context set, we viewed a brief clip of the George Floyd murder video, although we only watched the parts before the violence began. There are some things that my sons are simply too young to see.

During our next outing to the park, Shawn joined us as we played catch. Typical of the summer of 2020, we heard police sirens in the distance and helicopters above. At one point during our trip, a helicopter came close to our area and remained hovering above us. I suspected that a protest was moving in our direction, so we gathered our belongings and mounted our bikes to check out our surroundings. Soon we heard the faint chants of a large crowd walking in the southbound lanes of Lake Shore Drive. As they came closer, we heard their protests clearly: "Say his name! George Floyd!" "Say her name! Breonna Taylor!" "Hey hey, ho ho, these racist cops have got to go." My sons saw a multi-racial crowd of men, women, boys, and girls, some carrying signs with protest slogans or the names of the deceased, all marching peacefully. Just as the boys have kept the memory of Carole Robertson alive, those marching in the streets wanted to keep the names of Atatiana Jefferson and Laquan McDonald alive.

As the crowd passed by, Grant and Reid asked if they could join the protest. With their understanding that children can make a difference, they wanted to be a part of the change being demanded on the streets. This is how we joined our first protest of the summer as a family, riding our bikes down Lake Shore Drive. Later in the summer, the boys joined Shawn and her friends for a march down Martin Luther King, Jr. Drive. The protesters departed from Rainbow/PUSH headquarters on East 50th street, carrying signs saying, "Black Lives Matter," and "No Justice, no Peace." Nearby police kept them safe, with no traffic in sight. The boys asked their mother, "Are those police good guys or bad guys?" Shawn responded, "Boys, most are good guys, and today they're protecting our right to march."

Unfortunately, my sons will find themselves trying to discern between the good police and the bad police many more times in their lives because there is no magic spell to reveal who's who. A foundational element of American policing was the enforcement of unjust laws that devalued the dignity, safety, and lives of African Americans. While laws have changed over the years, like other professions and parts of our society, policing has an indelible institutional memory and culture. Anti-Black bias in policing remains, and it is especially problematic because of the power we entrust as a society to our police. The issue is complex and nuanced, but the bottom line is that it's my job to ensure that my sons understand the "ground rules" of police engagement and can get home safely each day.

Not long after the first protests of the summer began, my boys saw how Black protestors and their allies can be treated in this country, and this only reinforced the lessons I had been teaching them all their lives. On June 1st, 2020, a breaking news alert caught my eye. It concerned the thousands who had gathered in Washington, DC in the name of George Floyd, and when I turned on the news, the boys (who were homeschooling at that time due to COVID-19) and I watched in disbelief as police from various law enforcement agencies, acting under President Trump's calls to end the "lawlessness" in the streets, fired rubber bullets and tear gas at peaceful protestors in Lafayette Square. (Although there had been rioting the night before, the protest that evening was peaceful, with chanting and dancing.)[30] The chaos that ensued reminded me of the 1960s, when police routinely turned fire hoses and dogs on Civil

30 The Washington Post: <https://wapo.st/3MHy3sp>

Rights protestors who were exercising their rights to assembly and free speech. 2020 was five decades distant from the 1960s, yet the handling of the situation was emblematic of the disproportionate force that law enforcement reflexively unleashes to keep African Americans and their allies in their place. My boys watched as hundreds of defenseless protestors were violently pushed out of Lafayette Square, their dignified cries for justice and righteousness met with suppressive force.

I teach my sons to react calmly and respectfully to the police because there is no denying that Black people and white people are treated very differently by law enforcement in this country. There are countless historical examples, but this was once again illustrated to me on January 6, 2021. I began the day with optimism given the results of the historic US Senate runoff elections in Georgia the night before; Raphael Warnock became the first African American US senator from Georgia.[31] But by the afternoon, that high had been dissolved by an unfolding reality check: the insurrection at the US Capitol.

Much like the crowds of people who opposed the marches and sit-ins of the Civil Rights Movement, individuals who believed that America was off course and that her best days would remain behind her without action showed up in Washington, DC to realize their vision. The predominantly white crowd gathered to protest the 2020 presidential election results; they were addressed by President Trump among others. They marched to the Capitol, with the intent of stopping our legislators from performing their duties to certify the election of president-elect Joseph Biden and vice president-elect Kamala Harris.[32]

31 The Guardian: <https://bit.ly/3LwrR6u>
32 The Britannica Group: <https://bit.ly/39kpuFC>

Flying Confederate flags, wearing body armor, carrying weapons,[33] wearing gas masks, this mob breached the Capitol building and laid siege to the institutions of our democracy. Watching this travesty unfold, Shawn, the boys, and I were glued to the television like much of the nation. My children couldn't believe that the Capitol was under attack and found it hard to understand that adults could behave this way, with symbols of hate proudly displayed. And one truth in particular puzzled them: the police were so few in numbers despite extremist Trump supporters literally climbing the facade of the Capitol.

After watching so many months of Black Lives Matter protests all across the nation, Grant and Reid were familiar with militarized police forces: armored vehicles; canisters of tear gas; mounted police; canine units; rubber bullets; and helicopters above. Yet law enforcement's response to a predominately white mob's insurrection that trashed the U.S. Capitol, endangered the lives of our legislators, and threatened national security was impotent and utterly disproportionate to the threat. Yet too many African Americans have been killed by law enforcement for doing far less—sometimes just for being Black. Unarmed Black men running from the police have been shot in the back and killed,[34] yet during the insurrection the police took selfies with members of a mob who broke into the speaker of the house's office.[35] My sons needed to know that never in a million years would they be able to behave in this manner, even if their cause was just and right, and I told them this as clearly as I could. If the crowd had been Black and Brown, there

---

33 National Public Radio: <https://n.pr/37YuZJR>
34 WNYC Studios: <https://bit.ly/38H6Qr3>
35 Business Insider: <https://bit.ly/3P2usaH>

might have been a large-scale massacre, and hundreds would have gone to jail that day.

After hours of watching, my oldest turned to me and asked, "Daddy, are we safe?" I assured him that I would protect our family and that we would be okay. While both boys slept well that night, the following evening they called a family meeting at 7:30 p.m. to discuss their feelings and what they understood from the scenes they'd witnessed on TV. Listening to them share their thoughts and concerns, I was reminded how important it is to support the emotional well-being of our African American sons in addition to tending to their other needs as well. As a father, I dream that Grant and Reid, as they grow into teenagers and young adults, will use their education and mental fortitude to make our nation and our world a better place. Injustice, hate, and racism, as ugly as they are, have power, and in the words of Frederick Douglass, "Power concedes nothing without demand. It never did and it never will." I hope my sons, and other young people of their generation, make that demand.

CHAPTER 19

In the Midst of the Pandemic

A FEW HOURS BEFORE SUNRISE, I ARRIVED AT A LOCAL PUB IN THE Treme neighborhood of New Orleans to meet my fraternity brothers Lucius, Kevin, and Gary for an age-old tradition that we were taking part in as a group for the first time. We arrived at the bar at 3:45 a.m. on a mission: getting ready for the day's events. It was Mardi Gras morning, February 25, 2020, and we were invited guests who would be riding with the famed and historic Zulu Krewe on one of its firetruck floats during the parade. While our costumes wouldn't be as elaborate as other Zulu parade participants, having our faces painted was part of the tradition of the day. With several others ahead of us, we had to wait for our turns to have our faces painted, which gave us the chance to scope out the work of the makeup artists and sample the red beans and rice and chicken gumbo behind the bar.

By 4:40 a.m., I was in the face-painting chair being attended to by a young lady from Manhattan. While my face was her canvas for the moment, her regular job was doing makeup at CNN's New York City studio; clearly, she too had a Mardi Gras tradition, and I'm sure it was lucrative. We exchanged light chat as she meticulously painted my face in black with red highlights, first coating the area around my mouth and goatee in gold with red trim, and then painting a red diamond with white trim around my right eye. My friends nodded at me approvingly as her design progressed to their liking. Plenty of light banter filled the room as more people arrived at the bar to take their place in line and to get sized for their jerseys and other costume items for the day. Lucius, Kevin, and Gary each had their turns with my makeup artist, and we each got the same design. By 6:00 a.m. we were finished and ready to move on to the next phase of the day's celebrations.

We must have spent five to six hours on the float from the time we staged to the time we lined up and began riding forward. It was exciting to roll through the neighborhoods of New Orleans, and I marveled at the energy, the colors, and the joy on the faces of the young and old alike. We had tons of beads and other throws that we tossed to the crowd almost nonstop. We also had the coveted, hand-painted Zulu coconut throws, and I loved passing these out. I knew how treasured the coconuts are—in years past, I had run behind many Zulu floats chasing coconuts and bags of goodies from friends who were riding. At some point during the parade, forward movement stalled right across the street from a Popeyes restaurant. One of our fellow participants jumped off the float and fought through the crowd to buy some chicken and biscuits for us. We didn't have much time to eat, but having a little something in our stomachs tided us over through the rest of the parade.

At the end of the route, it was customary for riders to disembark from the float and walk through the crowd. While there were many people on our float, the four of us, carrying our large knapsacks full of coconuts, decided to walk as a group through the crowd of literally thousands of people. Clearly we didn't have enough coconuts for everyone, so we began randomly and indiscriminately handing out these precious Mardi Gras treasures, although I will admit that I couldn't help but give preference to children. (The real winners at Mardi Gras are the children, as few can say no to an innocent child who's begging to be thrown a prize.) After about ten minutes of braving the crowd, we exhausted our goodies, and it was time to move on. We headed back to our starting point at the bar. From there, a few of us went over to the Zulu Social Club for an afterparty; I said hello to some good friends who were there, including my mentor, Dr. Ingrid Labat. I couldn't stay long, however, since I had a 6:00 p.m. flight back to Chicago. This trip had been bittersweet for me from the start, as usually my entire family would be with me for Mardi Gras, and we would spend time with our dear friends and mentors Grace and Dr. Romell Madison; however, I had adjacent travel on the calendar, so my trip to the Crescent City had to be very quick. Truly, this year I was on the ground in New Orleans for less than twenty-four hours, having arrived late the night before. The trip was so tight on time that I needed to go to the airport with my face still painted. I had to drop into the restroom before entering security to wash the paint from my face.

As I settled into my seat, I began getting caught up on the day's news, clicking through stories on various news apps on my phone. There were more and more ominous reports about a new contagion called COVID-19 that was causing significant global concern as it spread across China and other Asian countries. (I already knew that a case of COVID-19 associated with travel to China had been found in Illinois in late January, but the SARS-CoV-2 coronavirus was not yet considered a widespread threat to public health.) In the back of my mind, I wondered about this new virus and began considering whether I should take extra safety measures on the days when I worked in the emergency department.

As I headed to the office the next morning, the air was crisp, and snow coated the ground. News continued to flood in regarding the spreading virus, and concerns about an emerging global pandemic were gaining steam. I went about my day as I normally would, but later that afternoon, as I was finalizing my remarks for a speech I was giving on February 27 at the Mayo Clinic in Jacksonville, FL it began to sink in: this novel virus was not just affecting foreign shores, but it was likely silently making its way through the United States. There was much that was unknown about this coronavirus, but the idea of traveling to Florida the next day made me a little uneasy.

When I arrived in Jacksonville for the conference, caution was in the air. Hand-sanitizer stations were readily visible, and the chairs in meeting rooms were spaced wide apart for social distancing. I even found myself more vigilant than usual with my hand hygiene. Regardless, it was great to see many new and familiar faces in attendance. I took to the podium to deliver a vibrant presentation on increasing diversity among the country's physicians. I talked about the improbability of my becoming a physician and illustrated my point by showing an old family photo from the 1950s featuring my maternal grandparents and their many kids. I shared my perspective on intergenerational distrust of the medical community within communities of color, using as an example the sentiments expressed by my maternal grandfather, a sharecropper, to his sons over the years. My argument—that we need to entice more Blacks and African Americans into medicine and support them as they develop into doctors—was received well, and the audience saw how more physicians of color could improve access to quality, build patient trust, and reduce longstanding healthcare disparities over time.

Like water dripping from a faucet, slowly but steadily I began hearing about more novel coronavirus cases in the greater Chicago area and Illinois as a whole. Some four days after community-level transmission not associated with travel was detected, I found myself sitting in the emergency department ready to begin my shift. (Community-level transmission not associated with travel is an indicator that a virus is spreading rapidly.) It was always my habit to wipe down my keyboard and phone with sanitizing wipes at the start of my shift, but now this precaution felt inadequate. Undoubtedly, infection among those who had not traveled was only the tip of the iceberg for ongoing viral transmission, a transmission that was undetectable and spreading beneath the surface of our community. I had visions in my head of doctors in China who were protecting themselves with full body suits, respirators, and face shields as they were caring for sick patients with COVID-19. It was becoming readily clear to the scientific/medical community that, for the first few days after catching the virus, it was impossible to tell by looking at someone if they were infected and shedding viral particles. This begged the question, what precautions should I take to keep myself safe? Luckily for me, sitting on my desk were several prepackaged N95 respirators (N95 respirators are close-fitting masks that filter out at least ninety-five percent of airborne particles.) that had been left by the physician on the prior shift; I decided to put one on along with a pair of protective eye shields. I wore these for the entire shift as I went from patient room to patient room—so much protection felt like overkill, especially since most other staff were not wearing respirators or surgical masks. It wasn't overkill, however, and in the weeks and months to come, I heard of multiple instances of doctors and nurses becoming infected with COVID-19 from asymptomatic yet contagious patients they had seen for minor complaints like an ankle sprain or back pain.

In mid-March, while working in the emergency department, I cared for a woman who presented with signs of a stroke. It was sad because the stroke was massive, affecting a large area of one side of her brain. We performed an emergent CT angiogram of her brain, and in addition to finding the location of the clot, we also found a very large blood clot in a major artery that sends blood to her lungs, called a pulmonary embolism. I recall embracing her husband following a bedside conversation about her prognosis just prior to her being transferred to an outside hospital. At this point, we didn't have COVID-19 tests available in the hospital, and I didn't think one was necessary as my patient didn't have a cough or fever. However, in the weeks that followed, we learned about the tendency of COVID-19 to cause blood clots in various parts of the body, and I wondered if this lady could've been among the first COVID-19 patients for whom I cared.

In the next few weeks, a global pandemic was declared, and many communities across the country (and across the world) began to issue stay-at-home orders. Hotspots of infection across the country became pervasive, and then came the thousands, of daily deaths. Just over a month after Mardi Gras, I began to read news reports about members of the Zulu Krewe who had been hospitalized with COVID-19, with a number of them dying from the infection. Undoubtedly, some of these men had been in the bar getting their faces painted on Mardi Gras morning with me. There were also signs of massive community transmission in New York City, where my Mardi Gras makeup artist lived and worked. Given all this, I looked back on one of my most memorable trips to Mardi Gras and considered what could have happened. Yet again, I found myself thanking God for, and reflecting upon, His grace. After all, I sat face-to-face with a woman from Manhattan for thirty minutes while having my face painted, I spent the day hanging out with people from different parts of the country when riding in the parade, and I waded into a crowd of thousands of people, yet He brought me home safely, virus-free and able to help others as they struggled with illness.

Illinois was one of the many states that issued full stay-at-home orders for non-essential workers, and my subsequent shifts in the emergency department during the lockdown were sobering. The all-so-common visits for chest pain, stroke symptoms, back pain, and other ailments seemed to just disappear as people, afraid of becoming infected with the virus, began avoiding the emergency room at all costs. Instead, nearly all of the ER's rooms were usually full of patients who would've otherwise been upstairs in the hospital except all wards were full of COVID-19 patients. Many were on ventilators and seriously ill.

Due to nationwide shortages, personal protective equipment at the hospital was limited, which caused us to reuse N95 respirators. (N95 respirators are intended for single-use only.) Other medical staff and I adopted a rigorous, and even arduous, process for putting gowns and gloves on outside of rooms and taking them off after caring for patients, with the goal of not contaminating ourselves with the deadly virus. While most modern emergency departments have several negative-pressure rooms where the ventilation system removes air from the room and vents it outside, now nearly every room needed this feature to reduce the spread of the virus. With help from hospital engineers, entire wings of the emergency department were converted to negative pressure by reversing the airflow for rooms on the same ventilation circuit. With no time to build doors, the engineers draped plastic curtains in the hallways to seal off these newly created negative-pressure areas.

The Chicagoland area soon became a COVID-19 transmission epicenter, yet sometimes—despite how full our beds were—the emergency department was eerily quiet. I'd use these respites to document patient encounters and catch up on other paperwork at my desk. But then the silence would be broken by an eerie hissing: oxygen coming from the tanks under the EMS carts as they were rolled into the hallway and staged close to the secretary's desk. The occasional cough from the adjacent hallway, where overflow patients waited for a room, reminded me there was little refuge from the contagion. Patients were often without family and loved ones, as restrictive visitation policies were in place to protect the public. During ER visits, patients' family members were encouraged to wait in their cars in the parking lot, as the ER's waiting room carried a high risk of infection.

Many of our COVID-19 patients came from nursing homes. Clearly these vulnerable men and women hadn't been out in the community exposing themselves to the virus; in many cases, the virus was brought to them by healthcare workers, family members, and other visitors or staff who were contagious before they themselves knew they were ill. It was heartbreaking when elderly patients died without any family by their sides, but thankfully none truly died alone due to the bravery of the nurse, technician, or doctor who held their hand during that transition. Truly, COVID-19 seemed merciless against the elderly.

Too many older people were dying, but they weren't the only ones. Middle-aged patients with no clear medical conditions were coming into the ER and taking their last few breaths. One forty-five-year-old lady, sweating and gasping for air, came into the ER with severe short-ness of breath. Upon her arrival, we moved her from her wheelchair to a gurney in our trauma and resuscitation room, which is where we house our sickest patients. Within three minutes she was in cardiac ar-rest, and we were performing CPR and trying to revive her. I knew that her family was anxiously waiting outside for news, but now I had little hope that that news would be good. Despite intubating this woman, giving her multiple rounds of medications, and administering extensive chest compressions, we made no progress; after about thirty minutes of life-saving measures, I pronounced her dead. It was heart-wrenching. Although it was a short distance to the outside of the hospital where the family was waiting, it felt like a very long walk to me: I had news that no family member wants to hear. Delivering the news was as hard for me that day as it was the first time I'd lost a patient; it's never easy. One of my patient's daughters wanted to know why her mother had died, but I didn't have a definitive answer; however, given her otherwise good state of health and the high level of community transmission of the novel virus, I told her that her death was probably COVID-19 related. This suggestion struck a painful chord with the daughter, and she was vehemently opposed to the idea that her mother could have been infected with the novel coronavirus. In her grief, she told me that the hospital didn't have permission to put COVID-19 on her mother's death certificate—she even threatened to sue me and the hospital if we did. I explained to her that some coroners' offices were performing COVID-19 tests on deceased patients to provide better tracking of pandemic casualties; the cause of death notation would be out of my hands. With family around to console her, I quietly returned to the ER with my head hanging in sadness.

The need for evidence-based treatments for this virus was great, especially as we had a hard time making a real difference for those patients who were the sickest. Yet, the advice and guidelines from leading medical experts seemed to change by the week, and truly the best treatment for COVID-19 was prevention and not getting infected in the first place. To make matters worse, amid the valiant efforts of physicians across the country to save lives, an abhorrent misinformation and disinformation campaign was taking root across the nation; these lies were nurtured by those in positions of influence who put their financial and political interests above the health and well-being of human beings. The misinformation was so pervasive I felt I was in a public-health nightmare where influential voices were sending the innocent to be slaughtered by the virus. Since these selfish voices couldn't be silenced, the best antidote for false and misleading information was getting credible information from trusted voices to the public. As the weeks wore on, it became clear to me that the best way I could help during the pandemic would be educating the public about COVID-19's methods of transmission so they could take proper and informed precautions.

I went on to take part in scores of workplace and community presentations, panels, radio interviews, local and national TV appearances, and individual engagements with people who were scared of the virus yet distrustful of healthcare leaders and their recommendations. As better and more accurate information became available, my peers and I amplified our in-plain-language message so it could reach everyday people and persuade them to protect themselves.

The pandemic is still raging at the time of this writing, but thankfully we are on better footing now, as we have safe and effective vaccines for most age groups that prevent or blunt the impact of the infection.

N95 and other effective masks are no longer in short supply, and the wide adoption of their use has helped significantly reduce virus transmission. Emerging medications that reduce the severity of illness are offering promising treatment options for those infected. However, people are still dying avoidable deaths from COVID-19: many are wary of the vaccines available, while some on the far right of the political spectrum believe that not masking, despite the clear risk it carries, is a political statement. In the face of continuing deaths from COVID-19, there is still an urgent need for health education; only this will bring the pandemic to its knees. I will continue to be a part of the movement to address the needs of our nation.

THE 2020 SPREAD OF THE NOVEL CORONAVIRUS CREATED A GLOBAL CRIsis that challenged every physician to confront the limits of their skill to heal the sick. But doctors are human beings just like everyone else, and the pandemic affected us just as personally as anyone else. At various points in the first year of the pandemic, I learned of several dear friends who were struggling to survive COVID-19. I worried constantly about my family in Louisiana, which was another epicenter of the virus, especially as many of my people were older and therefore at high risk. I was thankful that most of my family down south were taking precautions, including masking, although I was often frustrated by my father's initial refusal to curtail his everyday activities or wear a mask in public. (The conversations we had, if the situation hadn't been so serious, would've been comical. Thankfully, I did eventually get him to mask up.) Even still, I was grateful that most of my immediate and extended family remained virus-free or had only mild courses of the virus. However, we did lose some family members to COVID-19; the first and perhaps most devastating for me was the loss of my godfather, Martell.

Just after noon on August 2nd, 2020, Danielle, my god-sister, called to ask me to speak with a critical-care physician who was caring for my godfather in Shreveport. At the moment of her call, I was providing technical support for a virtual meeting of the National Medical Association's Emergency Medicine section. One of my peers from the University of Michigan had just started his lecture and was providing updates on the latest research about COVID-19 treatments. I excused myself from the meeting, as I knew Danielle wouldn't call me unless it was important.

I was caught off guard by the call because Martell, having been released from the hospital several days earlier following a three-week stay, was supposed to be convalescing at home. In July, he and his wife, my godmother Lindell, contracted COVID-19, and while Lindell's course of illness was mild, Martell became very ill. Lindell, Danielle, and I had quickly developed a plan of action, and as Martell's advocate, I had had a constant virtual presence with him and his care team during his hospital stay. Alone on the COVID-19 ward without in-person visits from family or friends, Martell needed my help; it was my duty to cover the clinical issues for him. Based upon evolving recommendations from the CDC (among other groups), I made sure he had the right tests to exclude life-threatening complications and achieved lab values trending in the right direction. While this should not be the case, I knew that my engagement was making a difference in his care, and I did all I could to ensure that he received the best treatments available.

Once his oxygen levels were stable, and once his supplemental oxygen requirements were minimal, my godfather was allowed to go home to his wife on two liters of oxygen to continue his recovery.

As I spoke with the critical-care physician on the phone, he told me that he'd been called to the emergency department because Martell, after he'd been rushed to the ER with difficulty breathing, needed to be in the intensive care unit. The physician wanted to discuss advanced directives for my godfather as his life was now at risk. I had been on the other side of this conversation too many times as an EM physician; however, it was sobering and bizarrely different to be the one receiving such difficult news. We quickly reviewed Martell's prehospitalization status and his relatively uneventful hospital stay, and I indicated that his resuscitation status was a "full code," meaning that all possible measures must be taken to save his life if he stopped breathing and/or went into cardiac arrest. Following our discussion, I collected myself and called Lindell and Danielle to tell them how serious Martell's condition was at the moment. They were shocked, just as I was, because he'd been making good progress at home. When I called the hospital back about ten minutes later and asked for his nurse, no one was available to answer the nurse's line. Understanding how the ER works, I called back and asked for the unit secretary, explaining to her that I was an EM physician and urgently needed to speak with Martell's nurse, EM physician, or the critical care physician who had called me. She told me that they were all in a code, and I intuitively knew what that meant: my godfather was leaving this world. And so I sat quietly and prayed, then I waited for the dreaded call that I knew couldn't avoid. I had faith in God's power to heal, but I also recognized His grace; He'd sent Martell home to see his family before He called him to his heavenly home. So many people during this pandemic never had that chance, and I was thankful that my god-family had those few final days together. As I ended my reflections, my phone began to ring with the hospital number appearing on the caller ID; after speaking with his physician again, I then made one of the hardest calls I ever had to make. Throughout Martell's illness, my voice had brought comfort and reassurance to him and his family, but now I had to contain my emotions so I could get through a call I never imagined I would have to make. Knowing that my voice and words would be forever connected to this moment, I painfully shared with Lindell and Danielle that the ER team was unable to save Martell. While we knew he was in a better place, the pain of his passing was immense, leaving a hole in our hearts.

Today, I really miss Martell, although his departure created the greatest void for his wife of more than four decades, his only daughter, and his two granddaughters. He was a God-fearing man who served his nation in the United States Army, was active in his church as a deacon, and who, in the final decades of his life, served his community at the Good Samaritan Funeral Home in Shreveport. My godfather always had a careful, listening ear, and when I asked him for advice, he would lean back in his chair with a toothpick in the right corner of his mouth as I spoke. His words were few but salient in wisdom, and his actions were imbued with love.

I am one of the hundreds of millions of people around the world who lost a loved one to COVID-19. The humbling reality of medicine is that despite our advances in sciences and the broadening of our knowledge, there is always more to learn. Even when we believe we are in control and have the power to extend the lives of others through extraordinary and heroic efforts, we don't have the final say. Martell's loss reminded me of this harsh truth, and I remain grateful for the many years we had together. One of the ways that I've soothed the pain of his loss has been through educating and empowering others about the COVID-19 prevention methods we have today, methods that I wish had been available to Martell in the early months of the pandemic.

CHAPTER 20

Looking Forward: Working Toward a More Equitable World

My dream was to become a physician and use my hands and my knowledge to heal patients. While I achieved that dream, my journey itself expanded my goals, and I was driven to develop several areas of expertise beyond clinical care that reflected my new passions: pursuing health equity and setting more underrepresented individuals on the path to physicianship.

Before I had a working definition of health inequity, I knew what it was. As a child, I saw inequity firsthand in my own family. Some of my uncles, aunts, and cousins who lived in rural communities had limited access to clean water, safe housing, medical facilities, and transportation. And even for those living in the cities, household income strongly correlated with access to health insurance and quality healthcare services. These and many other factors—factors that ran deeper than clinical care itself—unfairly limited the health potential of the people I loved and cared about. Unfortunately, their experiences were not unique. As a physician-in-training, I worked across multiple hospitals in various communities, and I saw the stark differences in health at each: patterns of disease and injury that not only correlated with geographic location, but that were inextricably tied to race (due to residential segregation) in the Chicagoland area.

Certainly, the breadth of challenges that we must overcome to achieve health equity can't be remediated by any single doctor providing care at the bedside, but I remain dedicated to creating change. From speaking at local and national healthcare conferences to engaging sectors outside of healthcare, I've learned to use my voice to create meaningful impact whenever I can. I have aimed to share tangible ways that both individuals and healthcare systems across our society can make a difference in leveling an inequitable playing field, and I advocate for reducing unfair healthcare barriers that contribute to lower quality of life and shorter life expectancies among the disenfranchised.

Within healthcare, I have encouraged doctors in private practice, hospitals and health systems, health-insurance companies, nonprofits, and employers (who often share in the cost of health insurance for their employees or pay for healthcare services) to use a health-equity lens to evaluate and improve clinical quality. I believe that entities such as these, when they work together, can make a quantifiable and sustained difference towards closing equity gaps, and I give my time gladly and freely to help close those gaps.

I believe that supporting the most vulnerable members of our society is an important obligation. I'm proud to work with nonprofit organizations like the American Heart Association, where I serve on its national Diversity Leadership Committee, which examines the social determinants of health in disadvantaged communities while also supporting initiatives to improve heart health. (Similarly, when

I worked with the American Hospital Association, I helped expand its #123forEquity Pledge to Act program to more hospitals across Illinois.) I volunteer as a board member of the Cook County Health Foundation, a local nonprofit that primarily provides financial support to the Cook County Health and Hospital System, which is among the largest public-health systems in the nation. The foundation's commitment to quality healthcare for all aligns with my values, and the health system the foundation supports is a major safety net for those who are uninsured or underinsured. Additionally, at the state level, I serve on Illinois' Medicaid Advisory Committee, where, as a volunteer, I co-chair the Quality and Health Equity subcommittee. This subcommittee aids the Illinois Department of Healthcare and Family Services in meeting the needs of Medicaid recipients.

Despite safety-net programs, and even though the 2008 Affordable Care Act significantly reduced the number of Americans without health insurance, medical bills continue to be at the top of the pile of past-due bills in collection for the average US household.[36] At the start of my career, I never imagined that my medical expertise could be both life-saving and a driver of economic despair. For too many, the issue of affordability creates a vicious cycle of delayed care (for cost avoidance), increased severity of illness due to said delays, and higher healthcare costs in the end. Those in communities of color have a higher rate of medical debt in collection,[37] make up a higher share of those without health insurance, and have a lower average household income than those in white communities. As healthcare costs have continued

36 The Consumer Financial Protection Bureau: <https://bit.ly/3OPd5K8>
37 The Urban Institute: <https://urbn.is/3OPK4hv>

to climb over the decades, health-insurance costs for families and contributions to premiums by workers have grown. Each has shot up at a much faster rate than inflation, but no marker of increased cost is steeper than the growth in deductibles.[38] This matters because many American households are financially fragile, are economically stressed from paying everyday bills, and cannot handle an emergency expense of even four hundred dollars.[39] This fragility is higher in people of color and also correlates with the level of education within a household; those with graduate or bachelors' degrees fare better economically, while those with a partial college education, a high school diploma only, or no high school diploma have lower incomes.

There are certainly many opportunities to make healthcare more efficient, affordable, and fairer. We can better leverage data and information to improve quality of care, promote effective therapies, reduce the duplication of services, and lessen the waste that contributes to the cost of care. Both providers and patients, for different reasons, are often unaware of the price of any given healthcare service. This is in part because of the third-party component of our legacy framework for paying for care; there are perverse incentives in the system which can drive up costs. To mitigate this misalignment of incentives, there are many administrative processes in place to help keep healthcare prices reasonable, but they too can be inefficient and add avoidable costs to the system. While an enduring focus on these cost-cutting opportunities is necessary to make the healthcare system work for all Americans, we must concurrently address the upstream drivers of poor health and

------

38 The Kaiser Family Foundation: <https://bit.ly/3LEKFRg>
39 The Federal Reserve: <https://bit.ly/3FdS8nW>

disease that drive the downstream demand for care. I believe this must not be left to chance and needs to be a collective and intentional effort—we must address the inequitable circumstances that shape the lives of Americans today. We must take the long view and make the critical investments in clean air and water, quality housing, high-performing schools, good-paying jobs, safe outdoor spaces to play and exercise, and high-quality healthcare, so that communities will be empowered to achieve better overall health.

As passionate as I am about quality healthcare for all, I'm also deeply vested in access to quality education for all. I view education as an important catalyst for strong personal health, increased economic mobility, and self-determination. I believe that every child should have access to a high-quality public education. Unfortunately, the reality is that (not unlike many other social determinants of health) this is not the case. I've observed this both in my own experience as well as during my years of volunteering with young people at the Kappa Leadership Institute Chicago. Even when in the process of enrolling my own kids in Chicago's public schools, quality of education was certainly a clear and present concern for my wife and me as we began researching schools; we made a conscious decision to place our boys in the care of the public school system and to be invested in its continued improvement. Beyond my sons' education, I'm heartened to see local nonprofits increasingly offering high-quality pathway programs that are improving exposure to science, technology, engineering, the arts, mathematics fundamentals, and related career options for young people in Chicago.

Educational inequity isn't just in K–12 public schools. I see the glaring impact of it when I look at the number of African American, Latinx, and Indigenous physicians in practice today: each group is much less represented in the workforce than in the general population. Despite racial and ethnic population shifts over the last several decades, advancing racial and ethnic diversity in medicine has been painfully slow at best. For example, in 1980, African American/Black, American Indian and Alaska Native, and Hispanic/Latinx individuals comprised 11.3% of medical school matriculants; over thirty-five years later, in 2017, the same groups represented only 13.7% of matriculants, indicating an anemic growth of only 2.4%.[40] (Hope is on the horizon, though: in the 2020–21 academic year, this representation improved to 15% of matriculants.)[41] This lack of representation is not only reflective of the inequity of primary and secondary education, it also reflects the systemic obstacles—ranging from financial disadvantage to outright discrimination—faced by even highly motivated and qualified minority students who want to go to college in pursuit of careers in medicine.

Rectifying this inequity is a profound issue worthy of my efforts, as educational disadvantage has a significant detrimental effect on the health and potential of communities. While I haven't spent much of my time in academic medicine, I have worked to make a difference through mentoring students while engaging with leaders across the continuum of medical education. (Mentoring is necessary, but it doesn't improve outcomes at a significant scale unless educators and school systems are involved as well.) Additionally, for several years now, I've been working with the Accreditation Council on Graduate Medi-

---

40 The Association of American Medical Colleges: <https://bit.ly/3ONs2fR>
41 The Association of American Medical Colleges: <https://bit.ly/374ELcT>

cal Education's Office of Diversity and Inclusion Advisory Committee. This engagement has allowed me to support the development of new programs that have a national impact on the training of resident physicians. (The committee also has the honor of recognizing trailblazing graduate medical education programs and residency training programs that reflect new best practices for achieving a more diverse and inclusive physician workforce.) The programs that we've endorsed help make graduate medical education more inclusive for all physicians in training.

In further efforts to stem educational inequity, I also give my time to the Association of American Medical Colleges (AAMC), an organization that has identified, in many reports, Black men as being among the most underrepresented populations within the physician workforce. I had long been aware of the AAMC's diversity initiatives, but in 2020, I was invited to join an AAMC-National Medical Association joint effort: the Action Collaborative on Black Men in Medicine. When I looked in the mirror and reflected upon disease and injury trends among Black men, as well as their lower life expectancy, joining the collaborative was an easy yes for me; today I serve as co-chair of the accountability working group within the steering core. By collaborating with other leaders across the nation, we've established a strategic framework for enabling the success of organizations of influence (i.e., colleges and premed advising programs, medical schools, residency programs, and others). Our work will help ensure leadership accountability and recognize those organizations that improve the number of Black men entering medicine.

Early in my collegiate experience, I was exposed to many examples of generosity through scholarships, many of which were funded by individuals or families to open the doors to higher education for worthy students. I understood how this financial support, whether big or small, could make the difference between a student enrolling in college for another semester or having to leave school due to inadequate financial resources. Stories of financial hardship for college students stuck with me, and even before I finished medical school, I promised myself that I, like so many successful doctors before me, would provide scholarship relief to young people seeking a college education. In 2021, I established the Dr. Derek J. Robinson Endowed Scholarship at Xavier University of Louisiana to make good on the promise I had made to myself. I look forward to seeing this scholarship support the educational advancement of young people, helping them realize their dreams, for years to come. While it will take both time and concerted action, I can envision a day when our workforce in medicine more adequately represents the diversity of the communities across this nation. I will certainly be proud to have been a part of this evolution. That is part and parcel to improving trust, empowering communities with improved health literacy, and advancing the delivery of high-value, equitable care. As I think about the future, I remain hopeful that our nation will make progress on these important issues.

Making healthcare and education more equitable while caring for the vulnerable and disenfranchised are among the most formidable challenges of my career, and I look forward to the many opportunities that will arise to advance these causes. Like those before me, I don't have any earth-shattering solutions, but I am certainly prepared to humbly chip away at obstacles to good health however and whenever I can, and I trust in God's grace to guide me as I move forward as a physician and healthcare advocate.

Photo Album

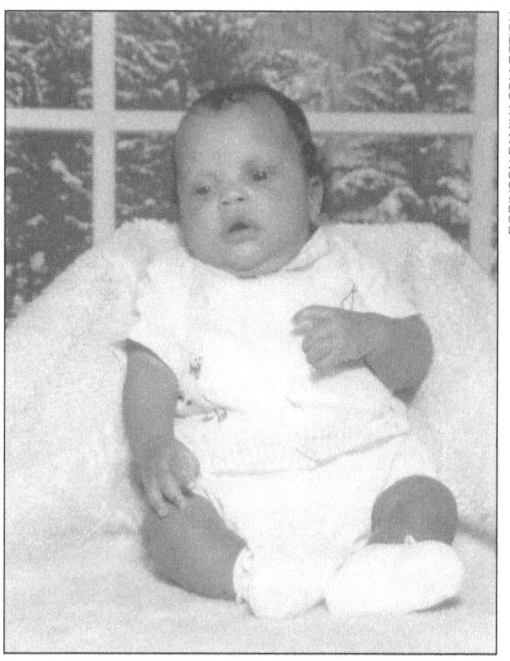

Me at one month of age.

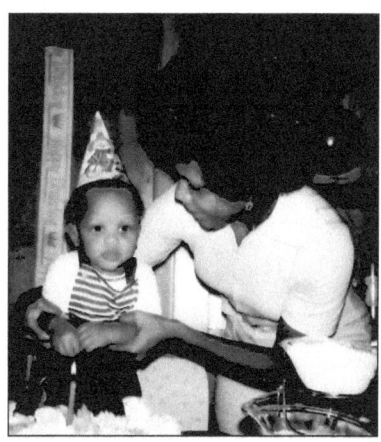

Me with my mom on my first birthday.

Me with my dad and paternal granddad.

Catching my first fish on the bayou,
sparking a lifelong love with fishing.

My swim team photo in 1993.

Historic family photo from the early 1950s of my maternal grandparents
and their children, including my mother.

Me (arrow) with teammates and coaches from City of Shreveport Swim Team in 1993.

Me with Xavier University of Louisiana's President Dr. Norman C. Francis in 1998, receiving the St. Katharine Drexel Award, which is the university's top service award presented to a graduating senior.

Receiving my medical degree from Dean Floyd Malveaux at Howard University in 2002.

My fraternity brother Rodney Gore and me with the young men of
the Kappa Leadership Institute Chicago.

Working my first Christmas eve
overnight shift in the ER as a
resident physician in 2002.

Following graduation from the
University of Chicago Graduate School
of Business in 2007.

Shawn and I were married on August 30, 2008.

Enjoying the Mardis Gras parade in New Orleans with Grant and Reid.

Robinson family in 2016. (Left to Right: Shawn, Reid, Grant, and Me)

During our family trip to the National Memorial for Peace and Justice in Montgomery, AL, I explain to Grant the monument to those who were lynched in Caddo Parish, where I grew up.

Poolside with Reid and Grant after I competed in the 2022 Illinois State Masters Swimming Championships

*Serving as the swim meet starter during an IL Swimming
competition on the campus of the University of Illinois at Chicago.*

*Grant, Reid and me on Chicago's DuSable Lake
Shore Drive for the 2021 Annual Bike the Drive ride.*

Shawn and me out for an evening dinner.

About the Author

DEREK J. ROBINSON IS AN AWARD-WINNING EMER- gency medicine physician and health care execu- tive who serves on the boards of several nonprofit and corporate entities. He was named one of the "Most Influential Blacks in Corporate America" by *Savoy Magazine*; "Top 100 Under 50 Execu- tive Leaders" by *Diversity MBA Magazine*; "40 Under 40" by *Crain's Chicago Business*; "40 Game Changers Under 40" by Ariel Investments and WVON Radio; "Top 40 Alumni Under 40" by Xavier University of Louisiana; and "Notable Black Leaders and Executives" by *Crain's Chicago Business*. He is the recipient of the Hero in Emergency Medicine Award from the American College of Emergency Physicians and the Leadership in Healthcare Award from National Medical Fellowships Inc. He is also a diplomat of the American Board of Emergency Medicine.

A Louisiana native, Dr. Robinson received his bachelor's degree from Xavier University of Louisiana, his MD from Howard University, and his MBA from the University of Chicago's Booth School of Business. He resides in Chicago with his wife and two sons.

WEBSITE

www.DrDerekRobinson.com

TWITTER

@DrDerekRobinson